Praise for Brassy Broad . . .

"For years Alison Bass worked as a courageous reporter for newspapers like the *Boston Globe*, attacking stories of financial corruption, sexual abuse, and pharmaceutical scandal in a dogged pursuit of the truth. Now, she turns her clear-eyed, honest reporting to her own story. Told with humor, insight, and a fierce, high-spirited determination to tell the truth, *Brassy Broad*'s inspiring tale shows what a lone woman who's unafraid to challenge even the highest authorities can achieve." — Karen Osborn, award-winning author of *Patchwork, Centerville* and, most recently, *The Music Book*

"During her storied career as a journalist, Alison Bass has exposed wrongdoing, questioned authority and held the powerful accountable. This page-turning memoir is a story of her grit and frustrations, her courage and triumphs. Bass shows us why journalism matters." — Eric Eyre, Pulitzer Prize-winning journalist and author of *Death in Mud Lick: A Coal Country Fight Against the Drug Companies That Delivered the Opioid Epidemic*

Brassy Broad

Brassy Broad

How one woman helped
pave the way to #MeToo

Broad

Alison Bass

Bink Books

Bedazzled Ink Publishing Company • Fairfield, California

paperback 978-1-949290-63-9

Cover Design
by

The May 8, 1992 and May 12, 1992 clippings are reproduced by permission
from *The Boston Globe*.

Bink Books
a division of
Bedazzled Ink Publishing, LLC
Fairfield, California
http://www.bedazzledink.com

*To all the female journalists who have come before me
and will come after me, our work is more important now than ever.*

Prologue

WHEN THE PHONE on my desk rang shortly before 4 pm on May 7, 1992, I thought perhaps it was a callback for a story I was working on for the *Boston Globe*'s Health and Science section. But no, it was Eric MacLeish, an attorney who had been a key source on several previous stories I'd written about sexual abuse. The latest involved a male teacher who molested several boys at a prestigious, private school in Cambridge.

"You on deadline?" MacLeish asked.

"Not particularly, why?" I responded.

"Well, you are now," he said. MacLeish proceeded to tell me that he was representing nine men and women who were accusing a former Roman Catholic priest of molesting them when they were children living in the Fall River-New Bedford area of Massachusetts more than twenty years ago. MacLeish said his clients were prepared to sue the Catholic Church if it did not compensate them for the damages they suffered at the hands of Father Porter, as the priest was known. They wanted him brought to justice.

Typing furiously, my phone cradled to one ear, I couldn't believe what I was hearing. Back in the 1980s, I had been the first reporter in the nation to write about how common it was for male therapists to sexually abuse their female patients. As a victim of sexual assault myself, I had tried to listen to the survivors' stories with an empathy that other reporters didn't always share. When I was approached by that very first woman with a harrowing story to tell about her psychiatrist, a well-known figure in Boston's healing community, I didn't immediately dismiss what she had to say, as one of my colleagues already had. That initial story in 1989 led to many others and almost by default, I had become the *Globe*'s go-to reporter for stories about sexual abuse by powerful men. So MacLeish's phone call wasn't all that surprising.

Nonetheless, what he had to say was explosive. This was the first time anyone had gone public with specific accusations of priest sexual abuse in the *Boston Globe's* catchment area.

"Wow," I said. "Any chance I could talk to some of the victims?"

MacLeish chuckled. "As a matter of fact, I have one sitting right next to me now."

Another voice came on the line. "I'm Frank Fitzpatrick. How can I help you?"

Fitzpatrick, a forty-two-year-old private investigator in Rhode Island, told me that he recalled an incident with Father Porter in the early sixties when he was ten or eleven. The priest, then in his late twenties, had taken him to a ballgame and to Porter's parents' house in Revere.

"He gave me some mincemeat pie and it had something in it that knocked me out and then he raped me," Fitzpatrick said in a flat voice. "I repressed it entirely until a little over two years ago, when the memories started coming back."

All Fitzpatrick understood at the time was that he no longer liked Father Porter and didn't want to be around him anymore. As a boy, he had greatly admired the outgoing young priest who taught at St Mary's School in North Attleborough.

Fitzpatrick wasn't the only victim who talked to me that afternoon. I also interviewed by phone a thirty-seven-year-old New Bedford man named Joe who had been hospitalized for depression and panic disorder and was now in a day treatment center for sexual abuse survivors. Joe said Father Porter molested him on three separate occasions when he was twelve. One time, the priest sexually assaulted him in his own home after asking his parents if he could go into Joe's bedroom to talk to him.

As soon as I got off the phone with Joe, I speed walked to the office of my editor, Nils Bruzelius, whom I respected and admired, and filled him in. Nils' eyebrows shot up.

"This is a great story Bass," he said. "Get it to me as soon as you can; Metro is going to be all over this one."

I would have liked more time to write the story but MacLeish had told me right upfront he had already given it to a reporter at WBZ-TV and it was going to air on their 6 pm newscast. So we had to get an even more thorough piece into tomorrow's paper. The pressure was on. After briefing Nils, I put a call into the Fall River diocese for comment. While waiting to hear back, I began writing. I knew I had to get the story over to Nils in less than an hour so he could edit it and ship to the desk before the copy deadline.

It helped that I have great powers of concentration, honed from growing up in a boisterous family of six and trying to read while my brothers wrestled on the living room rug right in front of me. Indeed, I was so good at blocking out the world when I needed to that my mom thought I had hearing problems and took me to an ear, nose, and throat doctor. He erroneously blamed my hearing difficulties on my tonsils, and at the age of seven, I had a tonsillectomy, all because I didn't always hear Mom calling me from the kitchen. I was also a fast writer and invariably knocked out my dailies well before the copy deadline. But this one was going to be tight.

The Fall River diocese never did return my repeated phone calls. With MacLeish's help, I finally reached a priest at St. Mary's Church in Mansfield, who was in North Attleborough in the early 1960s. He said he had heard about the sexual abuse allegations but only "after the fact." I also reached a spokeswoman for the US Catholic Conference in New York, who insisted that the Church took the problem of sexual abuse much more seriously at this juncture than it did even five or ten years ago. But she was vague on how exactly the Church handled such allegations.

I shipped a draft of the story to Nils slightly after 6 pm and he turned it around quickly, sending it back to me with questions and edits. I shipped the next version back to him within fifteen or twenty minutes. Nils or someone on the city desk inserted a paragraph about the WBZ broadcast and the final edited piece hit the rim just before the copy desk's 7:30 pm deadline.

Reading the *Globe* at home the next morning, I saw that the Father Porter story had run in the Metro section. But when I got to work, there were no messages of praise from the top editors waiting for me. Instead they seemed stunned by the allegations. On previous occasions when I had broken particularly newsworthy stories, I would sometimes receive congratulatory notes from the big guns. "Another fine effort in the Sunday paper—very thorough, very fair and we had the guy cold," wrote Ben Taylor, then executive editor of the paper his family owned (he would become publisher in 1996), referring to one of the stories I had broken about psychiatrists who violated their ethical codes of conduct by having sex with their patients.

But this time, there was only silence. I heard through the grapevine that Metro Editor Ben Bradlee Jr. was angry at MacLeish for divulging the story first to WBZ. Why, Bradlee wanted to know, didn't MacLeish give us the exclusive? I thought but didn't dare say out loud, maybe it was because he was afraid the *Globe* would bury the story or not run it at all.

When I first arrived at the *Boston Globe* in 1987, Jewish reporters there were relatively scarce, and scarcer still were Jewish editors and managers. The newspaper was run by Boston Brahmin Protestants (the Taylor family) and Irish Catholics, a mafia which pretty much mirrored Boston's inner power circles. Like myself, most of the Jews who did work for the paper did not have overtly Jewish names, with a few notable exceptions such as Ellen Goodman, an award-winning columnist who came from a prominent local family. Even though I was doing well at the *Globe*, I still felt like an outlier and so apparently did many of my Jewish colleagues. Early in my tenure at the paper, I attended a meeting of Jewish employees who all agreed we felt marginalized—not only by all the Christmas decorations sprinkled throughout the *Globe* building on Morrissey Boulevard—but by a corporate culture that did not include us in its decision-making and seemed uncomfortable with the way some of us expressed ourselves. (As a rule, we tended to be more outspoken than our non-Jewish counterparts). At the meeting, we drafted a memo outlining our concerns and an edited version was sent to the *Globe*'s management. Within days, a Chanukah menorah was added to the holiday decorations, but beyond that, not much changed. So when I broke the Father Porter story and proceeded to write several more articles about other victims of Father Porter, I felt distinctly uncomfortable, as though there was a bullseye on my back. Here I was, a Jew writing about the Catholic Church, which for decades in Boston had been an institution the newspaper did not take on lightly, if at all. In journalistic parlance, the Church was known as "a sacred cow" and up till then had been treated with kid gloves by the *Globe's* top editors.

The cow was no longer sacred. By mid-May, other reporters had joined me in reporting on various aspects of the Father Porter story. Dolores Kong wrote a piece about how some experts on sexual abuse felt the Catholic Church was not responding to the problem of pedophile priests as aggressively as other religious denominations did. David Arnold, a Metro reporter, did a man-on-the-street piece about how Father Porter's transgressions were the talk of the town in North Attleborough. And Kay Longscope covered a Church event in which she quoted the head of the Boston Archdiocese, Cardinal Bernard Law, saying that priests who commit sexual acts against children and adolescents were "the rare exception" and a "betrayal" to the faithful.

In retrospect, I think top Church officials in Boston were caught by surprise at our aggressive reporting on the Father Porter case. That might explain why Law castigated the news media, and the *Boston Globe* in particular, for what he considered sensationalistic coverage of the case. He even called down God's wrath on the newspaper. At an antiviolence march in Boston May 23, 1992, Law said, "The papers like to focus on the faults of a few . . . We deplore that. By all means we call down God's power on the media, particularly the *Globe*."

Reading those words in the paper the next day, I felt a shiver run down my spine. I don't know whether Law knew that none of the reporters currently covering the Father Porter story were Catholic but there was no question he was sending a strong message to the paper's editors, many of whom were Catholic (including our editor-in-chief): back off or be forever damned. Since I didn't believe in a vengeful Christian God, I wasn't worried about my soul. An editor at one of my first newspaper gigs had told me that if an article about a controversial topic didn't piss someone off, I was doing something wrong. Well, our coverage of the priest abuse scandal was definitely pissing off Cardinal Law. Personally, I couldn't care less what the good cardinal thought. I had gotten into journalism because I wanted to make a difference, change the world into a better place. I considered shining the spotlight on priests who took advantage of vulnerable children an important part of that mission. I was, however, concerned about my standing at the paper. As a Jew covering the Father Porter story, was I sabotaging my career at the *Globe*?

In the midst of all this tumult, I flew home to Pennsylvania to spend a few days with my parents. My mother had been hospitalized for an emergency hysterectomy and I wanted to check up on her. For the first eighteen years of my life and beyond, "home" had been Bryn Gweled, an intentional community nestled on verdant farmland about twenty minutes northeast of Philadelphia. Bryn Gweled was founded in 1940 by Quakers who envisioned a rural utopia where members who shared similar values about the importance of diversity and sustainable living could live together in self-governing harmony. Now, fifty-two years later, Bryn Gweled remained a flourishing intentional community with seventy houses, each sprawled across a two-acre lot, a heavily used community center and pool, and acres of bountiful woods and meandering streams.

During dinner one evening, I shared what was going on at work with my parents.

"I feel kind of uncomfortable writing about these priests who abuse children," I said. "It's very clear that some of our top editors, who are Catholic, are not happy with the coverage, although our Metro Editor is certainly gung-ho. Do you think I should stay on this story? There are so many other issues I want to cover."

Mom, who was a writer herself, nodded sympathetically.

"You should do what you think is right, darling," she said. "You have such good instincts."

Her words warmed me inside. She always knew what to say to make me feel better. Mom believed her four kids could accomplish anything, and she had always been my biggest fan.

It felt good to be home. The next day, I took a long walk around the circle, what my family called the one-point-five-mile loop of road starting at our house and winding around the woods across from our home in a large oval. The weather was cool but I didn't care. I borrowed an old sweater of my dad's and walked briskly, enjoying the sweet smell of the honeysuckle bushes that lined the side of the road and the azaleas bursting into bloom. For the first time in a long time, I felt buoyantly happy and at peace. The last thing on my mind was the fact that I would be returning to a city and a newsroom about to be torn apart by the Catholic clergy sexual abuse scandal.

Chapter One

"YOU DIRTY JEW!" I was around eight years old when I first heard those words. But it wouldn't be the last time. When I was in third grade, my mom and another mother who lived in Bryn Gweled became plaintiffs in a lawsuit challenging the distribution of the Gideon Bibles in our local schools. Bryn Gweled was an oasis of sorts, an unusually progressive and diverse community surrounded by mostly white, Christian and more conservative suburbs. The vast majority of parents who lived in Upper Southampton Township had no problems with Bibles in the schools, just as they had no problem with their children being required to stand and chant the Lord's Prayer every morning before the Pledge of Allegiance. I was the only one in my class at Shelmire Elementary School who didn't recite the Lord's Prayer. I just stood there in awkward silence, feeling like an alien and trying to ignore the baffled looks classmates shot my way.

The Gideon Bible case was the brainchild of Betty Polster, a Quaker who lived down the road from us in Bryn Gweled. She was married to Norm, an unobservant Jew who, like my dad, worked as an engineer. The Polsters had four kids, and they lived on a hill in an unkempt house with goats and chickens running all over the place. Betty had no time for housekeeping. She was too busy trying to change the world. But first she settled for changing our schools. A high school student in Abington, PA had already filed a lawsuit challenging the recitation of the Lord's Prayer in schools as a violation of the First Amendment (which mandates freedom of religion.) So Betty, with the help of the local ACLU, decided to file a lawsuit challenging the distribution of Bibles in schools, also on First Amendment grounds. She convinced my mother to sign on as the second plaintiff.

My third-grade classmates were probably too young to understand what their parents were talking about when they expressed outrage at this unholy lawsuit. But my older sister Linda's fifth-grade classmates were just old enough to get it and one day she was called a dirty Jew in school. She came home crying and Mom was furious. That afternoon, Mom took my younger brother Paul and me aside and told us that we were to tell her if anyone used such an ugly epithet with us. We nodded somberly and ran out the front door to play.

We were running down the driveway when Paul, who was a year younger than me, suddenly wheeled around, a devilish smile splitting his face.

"You dirty Jew!" he yelled.

My mouth dropped open; he had just uttered the very words that Mom admonished us about. "You are so bad!" I sputtered. Paul cackled; he liked getting a rise out of me. I clenched my teeth and ran back in the house.

"Mom," I yelled. "Do you know what Paul just said to me?" When I told her, she shook her head wearily.

"That little devil," she said. That evening, Paul got a hiding when my father came home.

My parents didn't take religious discrimination lightly. Indeed, that was one of the reasons they had gravitated to Bryn Gweled in the first place. Both of their families had come to America in the first years of the twentieth century as part of the great wave of Jewry who fled persecution and pogroms in Czarist Russia, which then controlled most of Eastern Europe. My parents grew up poor in inner city Philadelphia, subsisting through the Great Depression with the help of their extended families. When they married in 1948, they were hungry for something different: land they could own, a house they could build themselves. Who wanted to continue paying rent to absentee landlords for broken-down row houses in South Philly? But when they looked for property outside the city, they kept running into real estate brokers who said they didn't sell to Jews. That's when my father remembered a newspaper article he had read a few years back about an intentional community that apparently welcomed not only Jews but other ethnic and religious groups that faced discrimination. My parents fell in love not only with Bryn Gweled's inclusivity, but with its wide-open spaces and gently rolling hills. It looked like utopia to a couple who had spent their childhood living in cramped housing in Philadelphia's Jewish ghetto.

Almost everyone on the homestead built their own homes and even though my parents had very little money—my father had just started working as an engineer—they were determined to do the same. My father designed the house himself using blueprints he learned to draw in an architectural class he took as an undergraduate at the University of Pennsylvania.

Our family albums from the late forties and early fifties are full of grainy black-and-white photos of my father and mother wielding shovels to build the foundation of the house, climbing ladders to lay the roof, or carrying lumber that had been plundered by my father's father from junkyards around Philadelphia. It didn't hurt that Zayde Brager, as he was known to us, owned a junkyard himself in one of the city's worst neighborhoods. Although he was only five foot four, Jacob Brager, whom I knew as a kind, quiet presence, was apparently a fierce brawler when he had to be. I grew up on stories about how nobody messed with "Jake." He had once almost killed a man who attacked my father, then a teenager, while he was collecting rent on an inner-city property Zayde owned.

Once my parents started building their home in Bryn Gweled, Zayde Brager would rent a pickup truck and ride out from center city, used planks of wood, the rusty nails still embedded in them, piled high in the truck bed. Being a skilled bricklayer, he also helped lay the foundation for the house. Almost every other weekend, he and my grandmother would drive out to help my parents, or in the case of my grandmother, ensconce herself in one of our living room chairs and order everyone else around.

By the time I came along and was old enough to look around, our house was three-quarters finished. It was a multilevel Bauhaus knockoff with three bedrooms (eventually four), two bathrooms, and floor-to-ceiling windows in the living room and lower-level den that provided expansive views of the homestead. Off the front foyer in the den, my father had constructed a weird-looking, funnel-shaped fireplace that threw an amazing amount of heat into the living and dining areas and came in handy during power outages. If the power went out, and it often did in those years of heavy snowstorms and faulty power lines, we just camped out near the fireplace, which doubled as a cooking hearth and source of warmth for the entire family.

In addition to helping Dad build our house, Mom was also producing children. She gave birth to the four of us in the span of six years. She always insisted those years were the happiest of her life. They were certainly the busiest, since my father was rarely around. He worked all day and in the evenings after dinner he would retire to his den to study (he was always taking classes toward one master's degree or another) or play with his ham radio. He pretty much left the child rearing to my mother, but she didn't seem to mind. And that wasn't all she did. Shortly after I was born, she became involved with the local Democratic Party, and in 1954, was elected Democratic committeewoman for Upper Southampton Township, a position she held for the next sixty years.

When we were a little older, Mom volunteered her time as a lifeguard and swim instructor at the BG pool. Many of the BG mothers in this era of stay-at-home moms did similar volunteer work inside and outside the homestead. And a few, like my mom and Betty Polster, actively challenged the status quo.

After Linda was called a dirty Jew at school, my dad tried to talk Mom into dropping her involvement in the Gideon Bible case. But Linda's experience only stiffened Mom's resolve. She refused to take her name off the lawsuit. The case wound its way up to the federal court of appeals before it was rendered moot by the 1963 Supreme Court ruling that prayers and other religious artifacts in the public schools violated the First Amendment. Along with many of our BG neighbors, Mom celebrated that victory. But I think she secretly wished her Gideon Bible case had been the one that had made it to the nation's highest court. I was just happy that I no longer had to stand up in class every day, the mute other, as my classmates recited the Lord's Prayer.

Chapter Two

ONE DAY IN February 1989, I was working at my desk when I looked up to find someone staring at me intently. It was Chris Robb, a longtime writer for the Living section.

"Got a minute?" she said.

"Sure," I replied. "What's up?" I wondered what this was about. I had been hired by the *Boston Globe* two years earlier to cover science and technology but had recently switched beats. I had always been fascinated by human behavior and when the previous mental health reporter retired, I asked if I could take over her beat. While I had gotten one or two nice emails from Chris praising a story I wrote on my new beat, I didn't really know her. In response to my question, Chris looked around. I shared the paneled-off space in which I worked with several health and science colleagues, and one of them was eyeing Chris with eagle-eyed curiosity.

"Can you take a walk with me?" she asked.

As we strolled down a long hallway, Chris, who had long graying hair braided down her back, explained that a therapist she knew was counseling a woman who had been sexually abused by a prominent psychiatrist known for using alternative forms of healing in his practice. The woman, Chris said, had sued the psychiatrist, Dr. Richard Ingrasci, for malpractice and settled the case (for $15,000) a month ago. But she was concerned that Ingrasci was still sexually abusing other women in his practice. She had called another *Globe* reporter, offering her the story as an off-the-record source. But this reporter had immediately called Ingrasci, who denied everything. As a result, my colleague decided not to pursue the story.

Chris looked me in the eye. "Would you be willing to meet with this woman and her current therapist and hear her out? She is very credible and I think you would do a great service in exposing this guy."

Yikes, I thought. This was going to be tricky. The reporter who had dropped the ball was a friend of mine and an experienced journalist who would not take kindly to a younger colleague stepping on her toes. But being a sexual assault survivor myself, I felt like I should at least hear this woman out. I did a quick clip search and discovered the *Globe* had never written about sexual abuse by health care professionals before. This was two years before Anita Hill stepped up to testify against Clarence Thomas and many reporters wouldn't take the word of a woman, especially a mental health patient, over that of a respected health professional, especially in the absence of corroborating evidence from police or other authorities. In addition, the local media was still recovering from the backlash generated by the controversial trial of three Massachusetts day care workers for allegedly sexually abusing the young children in their care. All three workers were convicted in the mid-eighties and doing prison time, but by the time I stumbled across the Ingrasci story, they had appealed their convictions and there were rumblings in the press that the children's testimony was coerced and unreliable (the workers' convictions were indeed later overturned). All of this made *Globe* reporters leery of writing about sexual abuse complaints, particularly by women insisting on anonymity. And the allegation against Ingrasci was further tainted by the fact that it came from a woman who was troubled enough to seek help from a mental health specialist. The stigma of having a mental health problem was very real at this particular juncture, and some therapists used it to their advantage. Indeed, as I was soon to find out, several accused psychiatrists (through their lawyers) were quick to label their accusers as liars, fabulists, women who were clearly not right in their minds.

At the same time, however, I had been covering human behavior just long enough to know that false accusations of sexual abuse by women were rare. I understood that it takes a lot of courage for a woman, particularly a vulnerable patient, to level such accusations against a powerful man.

I nodded at Chris. "Sure, I'd be happy to meet with her and see where things go."

A few days later, I met the woman at the home office of her current therapist, Janet Surrey. Seven months pregnant with my first son, I had a huge belly that preceded me, and when Surrey opened the door to her home, she smiled broadly at my condition.

"You're still working?" she said. "I'm impressed!"

Surrey lived with Dr. Stephen Bergman, the author of the bestselling novel about medical residents, *House of God*, and a well-regarded psychiatrist at Harvard Medical School. Surrey and Bergman sat at a table flanking the alleged victim, a thirty-seven-year-old writer and cancer survivor, as she told me her story. Ingrasci was a well-known "New Age" therapist who dabbled in alternative treatments rather than dispensing traditional psychiatric drugs. When she went to see him, the woman says, Ingrasci fondled her sexually and massaged her in a procedure he called "vaginal Rolfing." She was experiencing anxiety and depression as a result of being diagnosed with breast cancer and Ingrasci told her that having sex with him was an integral part of her cancer therapy.

"He said cancer was about fear and that if I ran away from him, I was running away from fear," she said. "The implication was that if I left, the cancer might come back."

I was shocked at what this woman was telling me and found her very credible. She asked to remain anonymous in any story I wrote, and as I scribbled what she said into my notebook, I was furiously trying to think of how to make this into a story that *Globe* editors would run. I knew they would never publish one woman's accusation against a prominent health care professional, particularly when the accuser wasn't willing to go public. Not unless someone else could corroborate her story.

I asked the alleged victim if she had filed a complaint with Massachusetts Board of Medicine, which was supposed to investigate complaints about medical misconduct. She said she had but they had done nothing about it. I made a mental note to call the state medical board to see if I could get a hold of the complaint. I also learned that Ingrasci worked at a holistic health practice in Watertown, with several other practitioners. Perhaps someone there would talk to me about him.

The next day I called the state medical board and spoke to the board's spokeswoman. She said she could not disclose any information about an open investigation into a doctor, only closed cases. I asked if there were any closed complaints about Ingrasci. She hesitated and then said no. Her hesitation made me think that something was going on behind the scenes. I kept asking the same questions in a different way, but she refused to reveal anything to me. I then called the holistic health practice where Ingrasci worked and got the names of all four practitioners he was working with. I proceeded to leave messages with each one of them, but no one returned my phone calls. I then looked up their home numbers in the white pages and called them at home. Late one afternoon, one of Ingrasci's partners, a man by the name of Ted Chapman, picked up the phone at his home. I explained who I was and asked him if he knew of any sexual misconduct complaints against Ingrasci. There was silence on the other end of the line, and then in a gruff voice, Chapman said, "Let me call you back. I'm in the middle of something."

Chapman was true to his word. He called me the next day and said that he and his partners had reported Ingrasci to the state medical board after several female patients complained about him.

"Rick has a big problem, and he shouldn't be [working] in psychotherapy," Chapman said.

This was the breakthrough I needed, a credible medical professional acknowledging that he had reported Rick Ingrasci for sexual misconduct. My editor agreed and I started writing the story. It was early Friday afternoon, several hours before deadline. But before I had finished the story and hit the send button, Chapman called me again. He told me that Ingrasci had just surrendered his license to the state medical board. Apparently my questions had finally propelled the board to take action against him.

The board's spokeswoman confirmed what Chapman told me and my piece about Ingrasci's sexual misconduct appeared on March 5, 1989. After that story ran, it felt as if the floodgates opened. I began getting calls from other alleged victims not only of Ingrasci but of other psychiatrists in the Boston area. A research analyst for the Massachusetts

House of Representatives also got in touch; apparently her legislative group had done a year-long study that documented at least thirty cases in the last five years of Massachusetts physicians who had sex with their patients. I wrote a story about this study, noting that a bill was pending in the state legislature that would make sexual abuse by health practitioners a felony. A day later, I broke the news that the local district attorney's office had decided to launch a criminal investigation into the allegations against Ingrasci. In early April, I wrote an in-depth piece for the *Globe*'s health and science section about why there seemed to be so many cases of sexual abuse by therapists (research showed that at least one of every ten psychiatrists or psychologists became sexually involved with their patients). The reason, experts concluded, was that these therapists, who were always men, seemed to feel a sense of impunity because no one held them accountable for their actions. My article named a prominent Harvard-affiliated psychiatrist who was being investigated by the state medical board on charges that he had sexually abused four female patients.

The day after this piece was published, the sixty-six-year-old Harvard psychiatrist I named resigned his medical license. I wrote a follow-up story about his resignation and quoted another Harvard affiliated psychiatrist, a woman who was an authority on sexual abuse, saying, "Now this will encourage others to come forward. There are a lot of reasons victims don't come forward, but they include a kind of pessimism and cynicism and fear that no one will believe them or do anything about it. This is a very healthy development because it shows that society is willing to take complaints seriously and take some action."

Before I had a chance to find out if she was right, I went on maternity leave. I had met my husband, Jim, at a Boston Ski and Sports event, and on our very first date, we played tennis. Unlike my first husband, Jim, who was an excellent tennis player, was gentle and encouraging as he helped me understand the finer points of the game. We married in August 1988 and our son, David, arrived nine months later. I forgot all about therapist sexual abuse as I plunged into the joys and stresses of first-time motherhood.

Chapter Three

I ALWAYS LOOKED forward to the flashes of colorful chrome that greeted me as I skipped down the hill to Vanessa's house. When I was eight years old, Vanessa, a sweet African American girl whose father was the descendent of slaves, was my best friend. She wasn't allowed to venture off her property except to go to school so if I wanted to play with Vanessa, I had to go to her. By the time I rounded the last bend to her house, I could see glimpses of bright pink, blue, and black cars resting on cinderblocks near the top of the driveway, their gleaming front fenders grinning down at me. They made me think of second chances and new beginnings. Under the large capable hands of Vanessa's father, those cars, I imagined, would one day rise up off their ugly cement blocks and rumble back down the driveway, the burnished property of a proud new owner. Some of them eventually were moved, whether by tow truck or on their own steam, I don't know. I do know they were soon replaced by other jacked-up hunks of metal that Vanessa's father, a mechanic and part-time preacher, spent hours tinkering with. While the adults in our community viewed these metal carcasses as an eyesore—I know my parents did—I saw the cars as decorative, a garden of pink, blue, and black metal rusting in the dappled sunshine. And to Ray, Vanessa's father, they were something else altogether: a declaration of independence, a thumb in the eye of his oppressors. This metal graveyard was his turf, and here he could do whatever he damn well pleased.

Ray was a stern, solidly built black man who could make his daughters tremble with a look. With me, however, he was invariably kind. When I ran up Vanessa's driveway, I often found him working on one of his cars, cigar clenched in his teeth, a greasy rag in his hands. He looked up as I skipped past and taking the cigar out of his mouth, would wave it at me. "Hey there," he said. "How you doing?"

I felt welcome at Vanessa's house. Her family was one of four black families (out of a total of seventy households) who lived in Bryn Gweled, and my family was one of four or five Jewish households then on the homestead. In addition to the Jewish and African American households, an Asian American family lived up the road from us, and there was a smattering of Catholic and Protestant clans among the Quakers who predominated in those days. Class divergence was also not uncommon. Although most Bryn Gweled families were headed by professionals, there were mechanics like Ray and several carpenters. Then there was Elliston Morris who lived with his family high on a hill in an arresting Bauhaus-like structure. Elliston was a volunteer firefighter and a millionaire whose job was managing his family's assets. He could trace his Quaker lineage back to the days of William Penn. Just down the street from Elliston lived a janitor whose house looked like it might blow over in a strong storm.

We also lived on a hill on the appropriately named Hillside Road. Vanessa was the only girl my age within walking distance. Her haphazardly constructed home sat at the top of a steep hill, surrounded by trees, a large vegetable garden, and of course the carcasses of three or four cars.

Vanessa always wore immaculately ironed dresses, her shiny black hair carefully braided into two thick, oiled strands. She was not allowed to come and play at my house (except for special occasions like birthday parties). That didn't bother me at first, because Vanessa's mother always seemed so glad to see me. She had smooth high cheekbones and ebony skin. Next to my own mother, I thought she was the most beautiful mother in the neighborhood.

"Vanessa," she would trill in a high delighted voice, "Alison is here." She never called me by my nickname, Ali, like my own mother and some of the other parents in the neighborhood. And she always asked me how I was doing and listened intently to whatever I had to say. Unlike most of the other mothers, including my own, Vanessa's mother gave me her undivided attention. It would be years before I divined a possible reason why. This was the early 1960s and in rural Pennsylvania, a white girl playing with a black girl was a rare event.

Rarer still, I suppose, was a white girl's frequent presence in a black family's home.

Vanessa and I both had vivid imaginations, so we whiled away the hours playing with Vanessa's dolls and whatever other props we could find. We didn't have Barbie dolls in those days, much less Barbie dolls that looked like either Vanessa or me. But Vanessa had a cherished homemade doll with dark braids that looked much like her own. Her favorite game was dressing up her doll with bits of precious fabric cadged from her mother (Vanessa's mom had a sewing machine and made many of her daughters' clothes). My favorite game was pretending to be a bad guy who stripped off those clothes and made off with the naked damsel in distress. One afternoon, we were playing a variant of this game in Vanessa's bedroom when she simply refused to hand over her doll to me. I guess we were loud enough to attract Vanessa's mom, who came to the door.

She didn't ask us what was going on. "Give her the doll, Vanessa," she ordered.

Vanessa looked up sullenly. "But, Mom, she is just going to ..." Her mother exploded. "I don't care. Don't be selfish. Give her the doll now!"

Vanessa handed it over, tears pricking her eyes. By this point, I didn't want the doll; I just wanted to go home.

Most of the time, however, Vanessa and I got along great, and we would become so engrossed in our games that we forgot the time and were startled when Vanessa's mother called us in for dinner. By then she must have already phoned my mom to ask if I could dine with them that evening (with four children of her own, Mom was only too happy to oblige.) Vanessa's older sister was twelve years her senior and had already left to attend nursing school. Vanessa's two other sisters were a good deal younger than her, so by default much of the housework fell on her. Her mother was a strict taskmaster. Once when I was invited to stay for an early supper, she ordered Vanessa to set the table but would not let me help. I was consigned to the living room, where I wandered about aimlessly until everyone was summoned to the table.

Vanessa's parents didn't appear to have a lot of money. Her mother didn't work and her father only seemed to take on odd jobs. I recall sitting on a bench at their dining room table on the evenings I came to supper. The food was simple but there was always plenty of it. Vanessa's father said grace at the beginning of the meal, a ritual that I enjoyed since my own family just dove in and jostled for the plates of food as soon as they landed on the table.

"How is school?" Vanessa's mother would ask me as she ladled out the food. And off I would go, running at the mouth while Vanessa and her younger sister listened and ate silently. Vanessa's father also sat silently through much of the meal and as soon as it was over, he would disappear outside to light up one of his cigars.

In time, I grew uncomfortable with the strictures placed on Vanessa's activities and something else I couldn't quite name. I gradually stopped going over to Vanessa's house, although I still invited her to my birthday parties—my mother saw to that. By the time I turned nine or ten, I had found more compatible friends on the homestead—with the same freedom to roam that I had. But the easy camaraderie I shared with Vanessa and her family stayed with me, informing the interactions I had with other people of color. And those chromatic carcasses of metal in Ray's garden always made me think of endless possibility and freedom on the open road.

Chapter Four

IN 1980, I was hired as a reporter by the *Miami Herald;* I was in my mid-twenties and knew no one in Miami. No matter; this would be a new beginning, my first real journalism break. I loaded up my Honda Civic and drove down to Lorton, Virginia, where I took the car train the rest of the way to Florida. Two weeks after I started my new gig, four Miami police officers who had been charged with killing an African American man were acquitted. The year before, Arthur McDuffie, an insurance salesman, had been riding a motorcycle to his sister's house around 1:15 a.m. when police said he ran a red light. A dozen police cars gave chase and when McDuffie finally stopped, four white officers beat him unconscious. He died four days later.

When the acquittals hit the news on a Saturday afternoon in May 1980, the African American residents of Liberty City erupted, igniting one of the most lethal riots in the nation's history. I had been invited to dine with the Leons the day the verdict come down. They were a married couple with two young children who were friends of a friend of mine from Boston. They were the only people I knew in South Florida outside of the newspaper. I drove to their house in South Miami and returned that evening on Route 1, oblivious to what was taking place less than a mile away. I learned later that I was one wrong turn away from disaster.

The next morning, I got a call from Dave Nelson, the *Miami Herald* editor who was in charge of new hires. I was still ensconced in my claustrophobic room at the Bay Shore Hotel; my lease at Banyan Bay Apartments didn't start until June 1. Nelson wanted me down at headquarters to help with coverage of the riots, now in their second day.

"Bring your toothbrush and your towel; you may be here for a while," he said. Wonderful, I thought. If Nelson was trying to scare me, he was doing a good job.

The *Miami Herald* newsroom, a big open sea of desks, papers, and computers, seemed surprisingly quiet given what was happening half a mile away. A few reporters and editors, mostly white men, stood around in clumps talking to each other. There was only one African American face in the entire room. It belonged to a young photographer who came on board the same week I did. We went through orientation together. His name was Michael DuCille. He had a round, friendly face and was in his mid-twenties like me. He had just completed a master's degree in journalism at Ohio University and this was his first professional gig. The day the riots began, he didn't even know where Liberty City was.

Michael came over to say hello. He told me that when he and two white photographers, Battle Vaughn and Bill Frakes, had ventured into Liberty City to cover the riots the day before, all hell broke loose. At 62nd Street and 14th Avenue, Michael got out of the car to try to shoot some pictures. His companions figured the crowd wouldn't attack an African American. They figured wrong. Rioters started throwing rocks and bottles at Michael and the two photographers inside the car. Michael managed to get back into the car and Battle, a veteran familiar with Miami's back streets, sped away. Their car was shot at, its windshield smashed by rocks and concrete blocks. The three men inside escaped without serious injuries, but DuCille's camera was broken. All three were cut by flying glass.

Amazingly, DuCille was back for more the next day. With his wire rim glasses and neatly trimmed Afro, he looked young and nervous. He certainly knew where Liberty City was. I volunteered to go out with him, but the editors didn't think that was such a good idea. Instead, I was deployed at the City Desk, where I listened to the police scanner, watched the TV news for late-breaking developments, took phone calls, and fetched copy off the chittering wire machines.

The news staff was a little shorthanded—some of the paper's best reporters were still in Key West and Cuba reporting on what until Saturday had been the biggest story of the year: the Mariel boatlift. A few weeks earlier, Fidel Castro had thrown open the door to emigration in an attempt to defuse an embarrassing political crisis: the 10,000 Cuban dissidents who had taken refuge in the Peruvian embassy in

Havana. Castro said he would allow any disaffected Cubans who wished to leave to do so. They were free to go by boat from Mariel, a port town on the northern tip of Cuba, only ninety miles from the Florida Keys.

After hearing Castro's announcement, dozens of Cuban Americans in Miami with relatives living in Cuba rushed to Key West and were paying top dollar for charter boats to pick up friends and family in Mariel before Cuba's leader slammed the door shut again. Many of the boats, however, were returning to Key West with strangers. As Miami officials soon discovered, Castro had filled the boats with refugees from his prisons and mental health institutions, "undesirables" whom he wanted to get rid of. Over the next few months, 125,000 refugees from Mariel, 26,000 of them with prison records, would dribble into greater Miami and badly strain the city's social and law enforcement services. By May 17, the first day of the riots, 57,000 Marielitos were camped in makeshift tent cities in the Orange Bowl and the stadium's parking lot.

Many of the Marielitos with no family stateside would end up in the poorest neighborhoods of the city and spark a violent crime wave. Miami's murder rate would climb to number one in the nation. Among those hardest hit would be elderly Jews living cheek by jowl with Mariel refugees in cheap housing on South Beach. In the months to come police logs would fill with stories of old men and women being beaten and robbed in broad daylight.

That day, however, the big story was about the carnage occurring a few blocks northwest of the *Herald* headquarters. I listened intently to the staticky sound of dispatchers—fire at Norton Tire on 62nd Street, looter with a crowbar spotted breaking into the Allstate Office Supply building, black man shot in the chest at NW Fourth Avenue and 19th Street.

I couldn't stop watching the TV news replay about the Kulp brothers. They made the mistake of driving through Liberty City on their way home from the beach early Saturday evening. Jeffrey Kulp, a twenty-two-year-old passenger in the car driven by his younger brother, was dragged from the car, struck with bottles and bricks, shot, stabbed with a screwdriver, run over by a car, and left for dead, one ear cut off along with part of his tongue. A red rose was stuffed in his mouth.

His younger brother, Michael Kulp, eighteen, was also bludgeoned unconscious. A day later, both were still in critical condition at Jackson Memorial Hospital; Jeffrey Kulp soon died from his injuries. Michael survived but he was permanently brain-damaged. Jeffrey's girlfriend, Debra Getman, the third passenger in the car, managed to run down the street, where an African American man put her in a taxi to Jackson Memorial Hospital. She escaped with only minor injuries.

By Sunday afternoon, dozens more stores, factories, and cars in Liberty City and its surrounding neighborhoods had been torched. Miami firefighters, after coming under repeated attack by angry mobs, refused to venture into any area where Metro police could not guarantee their safety. "Let them burn the place to rubble," one frustrated firefighter was overheard to say. The National Guard was called in, and police and guardsmen were trying to block off the main arteries into and out of Miami's African American neighborhoods.

From the large plate-glass windows on the fifth floor of *The Herald*, we could see heavy charcoal-colored pillars of smoke stain the sky. The feeling in the newsroom was jittery; if the mob decided to march on downtown Miami, the Herald building was right in its path. At one point, a veteran reporter, arrogant with striking blue eyes, patted my shoulder and said, "Don't worry. If worse comes to worse, there's a heliport on the roof."

"Very funny," I replied. I was not about to let this s.o.b know I was scared.

By evening, police, backed up by the National Guard, had started moving, cautiously, to take back the streets of Liberty City. While thousands of people had marched on the Metro Justice Building on NW 12th Avenue on the first day of the riots, trapping police inside for an anxiety-producing hour, the crowd the second day seemed little inclined to challenge the perimeter barriers the National Guard erected around the trouble spots.

That afternoon, the people who died had brown skin. One of them was fourteen-year-old Andre Dawson who had followed his sister to a convenience store near his home. He was murdered a little after 6 p.m. when a white man in a blue pickup truck fired three shots at him. "They blew my baby's brains out," sobbed the boy's father on TV news. In all, eighteen people, half of them white, half black, were killed during two days of rioting.

By late afternoon, I was told that I could leave. I felt an overwhelming sense of relief as I drove back across the Venetian Causeway to Miami Beach. I cranked my window down a little and a soft feathery breeze blew off the water and caressed my face. In the distance, I could see the inviting lights of Miami Beach's storied hotels. For the first time, I was actually glad that I was on my way back to a hotel with a security guard and night clerk on duty.

MY COLLEAGUES AND I in the *Northwest Neighbors* bureau covered the working-class Cuban enclave of Hialeah as well as the largely African American communities of Liberty City, Allapattah, and Opa Locka. My beat was public education, and as I interviewed educators, students, and parents in those communities in the wake of the unrest, I developed a more nuanced understanding of what had caused the riots. The McDuffie acquittals were just the latest in a series of humiliating blows for Miami's African American community, which had faced housing and job discrimination for decades. Even the most menial jobs in Miami's tourism industry went to light-skinned Cuban exiles rather than blacks. Then there was the double standard in South Florida's criminal justice system. If a white man ran a red light, he would not have been killed, people said. Just three weeks prior to the McDuffie police acquittals, the black superintendent of Miami's schools, Johnny Jones, was convicted by another all-white jury of attempting to steal $9,000 in gold-plated plumbing fixtures for his vacation home in Naples, Florida. The Jones case was front page news in the *Miami Herald* for weeks before I came to town, and many African Americans felt that Jones was tarred and feathered because of his race. As I dug into my coverage area, I wrote several stories about how community leaders in Liberty City were attempting to rebuild their riot-torn community and prevent further bloodshed. I wrote about how parents were walking through the heart of Liberty City to knock on doors and urge other parents to get more involved and help improve the local schools. I wrote about how community activists had convinced Miami Dade Community College to build a Liberty City mini-campus for students who couldn't easily get to its main campus in downtown Miami or its satellite campus in North Miami.

I realized I felt more comfortable talking with educators and community leaders in Liberty City than I did with some of the white folks I came across in my professional and personal dealings in Miami. At one point, I went out on a date with a thirtysomething real estate broker named Tim and was appalled at his racist comments. The next day, I wrote in my journal:

"I think of Tim and how utterly superficial and boring he is. He typifies so many of the people who live down here, concerned only with themselves and their pleasure and quick to condemn people who don't fit their narrow norm. So many racists down here. If I were black, I'd soon learn to hate all white people. I'm surprised there are many who don't hate."

A FEW WEEKS later, I decided to look into a letter that a single mother who lived in Overtown, a narrow slum sandwiched between Liberty City and downtown Miami, had written to the paper. It had been routed to me since I covered Liberty City. In the note, a woman by the name of Dorothy Reese said the walls and floor of her apartment had jagged holes big enough for rats to run in and out of. Her three-year-old daughter had fallen through one of the holes twice in one month. But the landlord refused to do anything about the holes or the rats. I decided to see for myself.

When I arrived in Overtown that afternoon and got out of my car, an African American boy, perhaps eleven or twelve years old, started strolling my way, a shotgun slung casually over his shoulder. Other boys converged on me as well. I was panic-stricken, but I somehow knew enough not to show any fear. I ignored the boy with the rifle and strode over to a group of older men warming their hands around a barrel fire. It was January and the temperature was in the cool (for Miami) sixties.

When I gave the men Dorothy Reese's address, one of them pointed to the dilapidated, two-story motel-like building immediately to my left. By then, the armed youths had disappeared—they must have assumed I was some sort of authority figure, perhaps a social worker or teacher, someone who was there to help. I found the apartment and saw that it really did have rat-size holes in the walls and floors, a major safety hazard. I interviewed Dorothy Reese and left Overtown without any problems.

When I got back to the bureau, I made a few calls. The story I ended up writing noted that the Florida State Attorney General's office had filed criminal charges against Reese's corporate landlord months ago, charging it with 316 violations, including deteriorating ceilings, walls, and floors, broken windows and doors, and rat and mice infestation. But the case was thrown out of court because the attorney representing the state was not in the courtroom at the time the case was called. Would this have happened in a more affluent white neighborhood of Miami? Somehow I doubted it. A source at the Attorney General's office later told me that Dorothy Reese's landlord had fixed the large jagged holes in her Overtown apartment and done some fumigating for rats. I never went back to see, but being exposed to the horrible conditions that many poor families in Miami lived in, less than a mile from the opulent mansions on Biscayne Bay, left an indelible impression on me. I had never seen such extreme disparities between rich and poor before.

A few months later, one of my sources tipped me off to the story of a nine-year-old kid from Liberty City who had already compiled a lengthy arrest record. I interviewed his mother, a single woman on welfare with three other children from different fathers and obtained permission from her to interview her son and write a story about him, as long as I didn't use his real last name. I also interviewed a former case worker with the state's child protection services who had tried to help the family and a law enforcement official familiar with the boy's arrest record. The story contained verifiable facts about the boy's arrest history as well as my interviews with the police officer and case worker. But it was my bad luck that some weeks earlier, the *Washington Post* discovered that Janet Cooke, who won a Pulitzer for a story she wrote about an eight-year-old heroin addict in D.C., made the whole thing up. The *Post* fired Cooke and forced her to give back the Pulitzer. All of this made the *Miami Herald* editors very leery of my story. Over the strenuous objections of my editors from *Northwest Neighbors*, they refused to run it.

The editors who nixed it tried to explain that even though they trusted my reporting, they were afraid to run the story in the wake of what had just happened with Janet Cooke. I wasn't buying that. If they truly trusted my reporting—and my immediate editors, to whom I had shown the arrest records and all my notes, did—then what Cooke had done shouldn't have mattered. My story was as much about the failure of Miami's child protection services to keep a disadvantaged boy out of trouble as it was about how poverty, racism, and indifference can destroy a childhood. It was an important story and I was furious at the paper's top editors for killing it. I had a feeling that if one of the young turks downtown had written a similar piece, they would have run it. I felt humiliated and marginalized and decided to start looking for another job.

At some point, it occurred to me that I owed a great debt to Bryn Gweled and my childhood friendships with Vanessa and other African Americans who lived there. Those friendships deterred me from stereotyping people based on their race or skin. Unlike some of my acquaintances, I was not automatically apprehensive when an unknown African American male walked toward me on the street. All of this made me wonder: did growing up in Bryn Gweled help save my life that day in Overtown?

It also occurred to me that Vanessa did not reap the same benefits from living on the homestead. Two years before I moved to Miami, I heard that she died of a drug overdose in California. I sent a sympathy card to her parents, but I didn't know what to say. While the homestead was a safe haven for me, strengthening my ability to endure whatever prejudice I might encounter beyond its gentle hills, it clearly did not do the same for Vanessa and a number of other African American children raised in its midst. Bobby, a few years younger than Vanessa, also died of a drug overdose. AIDS took Stuart, and David, a boy my age who played soccer like nobody's business and had gone to Dartmouth on a soccer scholarship, had a nervous breakdown in his twenties from which he never really recovered. Perhaps these children of color would have suffered similar fates living in a less racially mixed urban environment. Or perhaps they just couldn't reconcile their cloistered upbringing in Bryn Gweled with the vicissitudes of racism in the real world.

Now, when I went back to BG for family reunions, I occasionally saw Vanessa's mother and father on walks around the circle. They still lived in the same haphazardly built house at the top of a long gravel driveway, and colorful rusting cars still littered their front yard. Vanessa's parents always hailed me with a smile and a wave, but there was restraint in their greeting now. I had an inkling as to why. I was a reminder of all that they had lost in the years since I came to play.

Chapter Five

OUR BUS STOP was more than half a mile from our house, and I hated the distance in the morning. It was always a race to make the school bus, particularly when it was cold outside and my siblings and I were loath to leave the warmth of our house. But the long walk home didn't bother me at all. I was in no rush to get back and sometimes detoured along the way—to poke around the nearby pond for snapping turtles or climb one of the tall trees that bordered the pond and see what I could see. High above the world, the meadows and wandering streams of Bryn Gweled homestead made me dizzy with delight.

On this particular afternoon, however, I'd taken the late bus home from school and I knew my mother would be expecting me since it was close to dinner time. So I didn't dilly-dally. Even so, I was surprised to see her waiting for me on the front steps of our house, her hands crumpled into the folds of her apron. By this hour she was usually in the kitchen cooking dinner and keeping a restless eye on my two younger brothers who were always fighting.

When my mother saw me skip up our long, unpaved driveway, she rushed down the steps and hugged me tightly to her.

"Darling, Beth is here. She's staying with us for dinner," my mother said in a strange choked whisper, looking at me intently as if trying to deliver some unspoken message. Beth was my best friend. We were both twelve and lived on the homestead. Beth was a tomboy like myself and we spent summers and weekends roaming the deep woods and meadows of Bryn Gweled. When Beth and I weren't making mud houses on the stream banks or swinging from vines in the picnic woods, pretending we were Tarzan rescuing Jane (we took turns being Jane but both preferred the role of Tarzan), we spent our time together at Beth's house, playing with her trolls or rearranging furniture in the amazingly intricate doll house that Beth's older brother, Geoff, made for her.

So I was not particularly surprised to hear that Beth was visiting. "That's great, Mom," I said and squirmed to get out of her grasp. But she didn't let go.

"Have you heard about Geoff?" my mother asked in the same strange voice. Geoff was Beth's older brother and of all the boys in our neighborhood, he was the nicest. He never teased me about wearing glasses and he let me and Beth play ice hockey with the boys when the pond froze over. Geoff was a Boy Scout and a star soccer player and I wished he was my big brother too.

Before I could respond, my mother added, "Geoff was in an accident last night and that's why Beth is visiting. But don't say anything about it to her—just be very friendly, okay?"

Hearing my mother's voice cut through the air around me, I suddenly remembered what Alan had said at the bus stop that morning. Alan, who was our age, was always trying to get a rise out of me. So when he blurted out something about Geoff hanging himself last night, I didn't believe him. Nor did anyone else at the bus stop. We thought he was just being his usual annoying self.

Now I wasn't so sure. I told my mother what Alan said and added, "He was just kidding right?"

My mother's eyes darkened and she twisted a strand of her sandy blond hair, which was loosely tied back into a ponytail. "I'll tell you what happened later. Now, let's go inside and don't say anything about it to Beth."

Beth was sitting on our couch watching TV in the living room, my two brothers sprawled on the floor in front of her, wrestling as usual. She got up when I walked into the room and just stood there as if she was waiting for something. I noticed that her usual ruddy face was blotchy and pale. I tried to pretend as if there was nothing unusual going on and strolled over to look at the TV. It was 1965 and we had a tiny black-and-white TV set with an annoying amount of static. But at least we had one, even though we were only allowed to watch it from 5 to 6 pm on the weekdays while my mother was preparing dinner. The Taylors didn't even own a TV; I got the sense they didn't consider television a suitable activity for children.

"What are you watching?" I asked, anything to break up the awkward silence between us.

"Superman," Beth said. I stepped over my brothers and sat down on the couch. Beth asked me how my day at school had gone and that's when I noticed that she was wearing faded dungarees and a red flannel work shirt. It didn't look as though she had gone to school today. I was afraid to ask Beth why she stayed at home and tried to come up with something to say, anything to continue the conversation. My mind was a blank until the television screen rescued me. Superman was about to save Lois Lane from that awful Lex Luther.

I pointed at the screen. "Look, Beth." She jerked her head toward the black-and-white pixels, startled by my sudden enthusiasm.

As Beth stared hypnotically at the television screen, I wondered what happened to Geoff. Like my older sister, he had recently started ninth grade at William Tennant High School. Even though he was a devoted Eagle Scout, Geoff had not been allowed to march with his Boy Scout troop in the Veterans Day parade the previous week because, as Quakers, his parents were opposed to the Vietnam War. But that didn't surprise me—almost everyone I knew in Bryn Gweled was opposed to the war, although we didn't make a big deal about it at school. In fact, quite a number of young men from Bryn Gweled registered as conscientious objectors to avoid being drafted. (The federal government allowed Quakers, because of their long-standing repudiation of war, to register as conscientious objectors and do an alternative form of community service.) One young Quaker from Bryn Gweled even went to prison for refusing to register as a conscientious objector because he felt it was unfair that he should be able to sign up for alternative service when other young men had no way to opt out of a war they didn't believe in.

The community outside Bryn Gweled was much more conservative than most homesteaders. While Bryn Gweled residents voted in a bloc for Kennedy in 1960, the Republican suburbs around us went solidly for Nixon. On the junior high school bus, I and other BG children were called "commie pinkos" more than once. The kids who rode the bus with us to and from Klinger, mostly the offspring of white working-class parents, didn't quite grasp the idea that adults in Bryn Gweled had jobs outside the community and that we only shared some common land. They no doubt had heard from their parents that we lived on a commune; hence we were commies. Once when I made the mistake of sitting further back in the bus than I usually did, one of the bullies in the back row started gesturing toward me and asking his friends in a loud whisper (that the entire bus could hear), "Is she one of them commies too?"

To my surprise, Gary, a beefy, round-faced boy who was a year older than me and hung out in the back of the bus, dismissed me with a wave. "No, she's okay. Leave her alone." For the rest of the school year, I harbored a secret crush on Gary, but other than an occasional smile or nod, he pretty much ignored me. Yet no one on the bus bothered me after that.

Other BG kids were not as lucky; Alan was a particular target for ridicule on the bus, possibly because he made no effort to fit in, unlike me. I was so desperate to be accepted by my classmates that later that year I ran for student council secretary (and lost). Alan's older brother, David, fared even worse. David, who was a year older than me and Geoff Taylor's best friend, had the audacity to write on a Christmas card for one of his eighth-grade classmates' father (who was doing a tour in Vietnam): "Merry Christmas but how merry a Christmas is it for the women and children we're bombing in Vietnam?" Word got out and a gaggle of kids cornered David in a hallway at Klinger that afternoon. Fortunately, a janitor happened by at just the right time and broke things up before David got creamed.

My thoughts were interrupted by my father's arrival—he came home early that night—and my mother soon called us to dinner. As usual, I sat at one head of the table, my brother Paul at the other, my parents to my left with their backs to the kitchen (so they could see the hilltop views from our large plate-glass windows). Beth sat to my right, and I honestly don't remember where my sister and youngest brother sat. Mom did most of the talking, telling us in a high, breathless voice about her trip to an auction in downtown Philly the day before. But no one was really paying attention to her. My siblings all stared at Beth in fascination, as if she was some exotic species from the Philadelphia

Zoo. Even Beth didn't really seem to be listening, although she nodded politely at whatever my mother said. I had never seen my friend look so subdued in my life.

After dinner, my father took Beth home, which made me feel relieved and guilty at the same time. Mom attacked the dishes with ferocious zeal, waving us off to do our homework as she always did after the evening meal. An hour or so later, I looked up to find her standing in the door of my bedroom, a sad look on her face. She beckoned me over to sit down next to her on the bed and that's when she told me. That Geoff was dead. That he had hanged himself from a noose of his own making—as a Boy Scout, he was an expert knot maker—in the basement of the Taylors' home, while his parents were out for the evening. Why? I wailed. Why would the nicest, kindest boy in the neighborhood, someone I wished was my own big brother, do such a thing? Why? I cried, burying my face in my mother's arms. But she had no answers for me, not that evening, or ever.

I didn't learn until years later that at a Scout meeting the evening of his death, Geoff had been excoriated by his Boy Scout troop for not marching in the Veterans Day parade, that he was made to sit in a separate room and penalized in some way. He came home, said nothing to his parents and then waited until they had left for the evening and his two younger sisters were in bed, to fashion the instrument of his demise. He was as creative and effective in finding a way to kill himself as he had been in making his way through his short-lived life.

Before Geoff's suicide, I used to spend a lot of time at Beth's house. I even preferred Beth's home to my own, in part because I didn't have to do any chores there. Beth's mother was always at home, a gentle, nurturing woman who made me feel special. She was invariably baking something delicious in the kitchen, her apron and hands covered in flour. Dorothy seemed so much softer and more accessible than my own mother, who was too busy to spend much time in the kitchen, except on the special occasions when she baked apple pies, the apples plucked from our own tree. Our kitchen was relatively small compared to Beth's kitchen and my mother typically shooed me out when she was baking or making dinner. My preference for Beth's house wasn't just culinary in nature. Most days when I got home from school, my mother was in the back of the house banging on her Olivetti Underwood typewriter. She would respond to my tentative Hello with a cheery, "Is that you honey? I'm back here," and then go right on with whatever she was doing. Beth's mother, on the other hand, always had time to hear about our adventures.

"How was thy day?" she would ask, using the Quaker pronoun for "your." And then she would actually wait to hear the answer. Beth once told me proudly that her father could date his lineage back to the time of William Penn. He was a lawyer who worked in downtown Philadelphia and there were rumors about inherited wealth. Yet Beth's family lived simply, as befitted their Quaker beliefs, and I always felt welcome in their home.

But after Geoff died, I increasingly came up with excuses not to go over to Beth's house. I was afraid of her basement, afraid of what I might find there. I had always been an imaginative child, prone to night terrors and the fear of darkness. I had nightmares about dark, creepy basements for years. Nor did I see much of Beth elsewhere. Shortly after Geoff's death, her parents pulled her out of the public junior high and enrolled her in a private Quaker school.

Up to that point, I had enjoyed going to Klinger Junior High; according to my diary for that time period, I thought Klinger was "neat." But after Geoff died, I no longer wanted to be there, mingling with the brothers and sisters of the boys who had participated in his humiliation. One evening after dinner a month or so after Geoff died, I lingered at the table after my siblings had gone off to play or do homework. My parents were finishing their dessert (and my mom her third or fourth cup of coffee of the day).

"I'd really like to go to George School, where Beth is," I said. "Beth says it's so much better than Klinger."

Mom glanced at my dad for support. He didn't respond. She was on her own. "Darling, you know we can't afford to send you to both private school and college. It's going to be hard enough to get all four of you through college. And it's more important that you attend a good college, don't you think?"

"But I hate Klinger," I said. "I'll help pay for college, I promise."

"I understand how you feel, Ali," Mom said. "But we just can't afford it. I'm sorry."

I was angry at my parents for weeks. I think deep down I was also furious at Geoff for killing himself, an act that essentially destroyed my close friendship with his sister and forced me to realize that the world had hard edges and sharp ideological differences that could ruin lives. As it turned out, Geoff's death was only one of hundreds of thousands of fatalities that could be attributed to the Vietnam War, the defining war of my childhood, but it had the most profound effect on my worldview.

I think Geoff's death and its aftermath set me on the path to becoming an outlier, someone who preferred to observe rather than join in. It is probably no accident that both Beth and I became journalists. We've spent our lives exposing wrongdoing and hypocrisy, perhaps in some small measure to expiate Geoff's devastating sacrifice. But all of that was yet to come. That year, I had just started writing in a diary, which my mom bought for me. My entries were fairly cut and dry, recording teachers I liked and brief impressions of school and friends I made in school. But then it stopped. My diary for 1965 ended abruptly on Nov. 16, the night Geoff Taylor hung himself.

Chapter Six

GEOFF'S SUICIDE HAD the paradoxical effect of radicalizing many of the Quakers who lived in our community, including his own sister. Once she started attending a Friends school, Beth regularly went to anti-war rallies, where she was joined by other Quakers from the homestead, such as the Polsters. Indeed, Betty Polster, who had brought the Gideon Bible case with my mom in the early 1960s, had become very active in the anti-war movement. She and various members of her family often attended anti-war protests in Philadelphia and Washington, D.C.—protests that Betty helped organize. As president of the Women's International League for Peace and Freedom, she even received death threats for her public stance against the war.

Up to this point, however, my parents hadn't gotten involved in the anti-war movement. As a first-generation American, my father retained a healthy respect for the government that took our country to war, and he had another reason for staying neutral: the electronics company he worked for had a lot of military contracts. My mom, on the other hand, was openly opposed to the war.

One evening at the dinner table, Mom started talking about how she wanted to go to an anti-war rally in Philly. She turned to Linda and me.

"Would you like to come with me?" she said. "I think it would be a good experience for you to go, see what this is all about."

I was sitting in my usual place at one head of the table with my back to the huge plate-glass windows that opened up to our back patio. It was warm out and Mom had opened the doors that led to the back yard on either side of our floor-to-ceiling windows.

Before my sister or I could respond, Dad shook his head emphatically. "You're not taking them to any anti-war rallies—they could get hurt. How stupid can you be?"

Mom flinched but said nothing. This was not the first time my father had put her down in front of us but this time it really got to me. I was almost fourteen and full of myself. I flung scorn at my father.

"You're the one who's stupid for putting Mom down like that," I retorted. I stood up, preparing to make my escape. I figured I could reach the screen door and run outside if I had to. But before I could make a move, my father jumped up and strode over to the couch next to our dining room table. He shoved it against the window, literally cutting off my escape route. We all froze, terrified at this brute display of rage. I was sure he was going to come over and hit me. But my father was so discomfited by his loss of control that he merely walked away and disappeared into his den for the rest of the evening. I burst into tears and ran back into my room. It wasn't the first time I had pushed my dad's buttons and it wouldn't be the last. We never did get to that rally.

While I wasn't an active peacenik like some of my BG friends, I didn't exactly run with the in-crowd at my high school, where many teachers and students were aghast at the anti-war movement. I wasn't really part of any clique, and even though I had made it onto my school's field hockey team, there were many times when I felt like an outlier. One afternoon when my field hockey team was traveling by bus to an away game, I heard the girl in the seat in front of me say, "She's just a dirty Jew." The hockey player sitting next to her looked back at me in horror and whispered urgently to her seatmate, who turned around and said, "Oh I didn't mean you." Shocked that someone I knew could say something like this, I could only nod, accepting her quasi-apology. I felt weirdly grateful that at least she said that much.

Besides being on the school field hockey team, I was also active in the Future Teachers of America club. I had no desire to become a teacher, but my guidance counselor said I needed more extracurricular activities on my college transcript; plus, the captain of my hockey team was the president of the FTA. So I joined the organization and by the spring of my junior year, it occurred to me that I was doing most of the work, arranging events, guest speakers, and bake sales to earn money for the FTA. So I decided to put my hat in the ring for the president's job. But on the afternoon the FTA members were planning to vote in an empty classroom after school, I heard another member of the field hockey team whisper loudly, "I can't vote for her; she's Jewish."

She was immediately shushed by the then president of the FTA, Gwen H., a level-headed young woman of German-Irish extraction who had just been named captain of our hockey team. I stood there, feeling like a blight on humanity and fighting to keep my tears at bay.

Gwen came over and patted my arm. "It will be all right. Why don't you wait outside while we vote?"

I fled to the girls' bathroom, which was thankfully empty, and tried to blot away the tears running down my face. A part of me wanted to quit the FTA and hockey team right then and there. I hated my classmates: how could they be so cruel? After a long time, I took a deep breath and looked in the mirror. I said to myself, "You'll get past this, Ali, I know you will."

I learned later that Gwen held an impromptu huddle, in which she announced that I deserved to be our next president and that everyone on the hockey team (which dominated the FTA) should vote for me. Fortunately, the other girls listened to Gwen—she had that kind of moral authority—and I was voted in as FTA president. When I finally returned to the classroom and was told I would be president, my mouth dropped open in astonishment. I couldn't believe it. At our fifth-year high school reunion, I learned that Gwen had gotten a job with the FBI. I thought but didn't say, they're lucky to have you. I have no idea what happened to the hockey player who didn't want to vote for me because I was Jewish. But I remember her name to this day.

Around the same time, I discovered some disturbing evidence that my high school was not the only institution that did not always live up to its lofty ideals. It had been almost a year since Martin Luther King Jr. had been assassinated and the African American members of Bryn Gweled were eager to institute an annual memorial event for the slain civil rights leader. This was in 1969, years before the nation finally got around to commemorating his accomplishments with a national holiday.

At a Bryn Gweled meeting, Perry K., an African American professor who lived down the road from us, made the case for setting up a committee that could plan a memorial event for King. But a number of other members, all white, spoke up against the idea. They didn't see the need for an event memorializing Martin Luther King. Finally, Perry stood up and said that he felt Bryn Gweled had let down its principles. He then strode out of the room.

All of this was told to me by my mother while we were walking around the circle a few days later.

"I don't see why we need a memorial event for Martin Luther King," my mother complained. "We didn't have one for Bobbie Kennedy."

I tried to explain what Martin Luther King meant to African Americans and the civil rights movement, but Mom wasn't listening. She abruptly changed the topic. That's when I realized that my beloved mother, who championed her own children so fiercely and fought to get the Bible out of the public schools, had a blind spot when it came to race—a blind spot that would only grow as she aged. This was also when I began to understand that while my mom was a strong, independent woman who believed her girls should be able to do anything, she came of age in an era when women were still very much under the thumb of men. It would be years before she finally stood up to my dad.

Chapter Seven

I HAD JUST sat down at my desk and switched on the computer when my editor walked up to me, a look of grim determination on his face. It was April 1, 1992, my first day back at the *Boston Globe* after a much-needed vacation in Florida with my husband and three-year-old son. Right before I left, I had written about the controversy dogging Dr. Frederick Goodwin, the nation's newly appointed mental health chief for making racially insensitive remarks. Goodwin had linked the violence of inner-city youths to the violent behavior of young male monkeys. One of his supporters, a prominent psychiatrist at Mass General Hospital, called my boss to complain about the tenor of my article. Nils was able to soothe the waters and he remained supportive of my reporting. But the constant second guessing got to me sometimes. My week in Florida was as a welcome respite from all of that. I swam in the refreshing waters of the Gulf, basked in the late March sunshine, and watched dolphins cavorting in the bay on a hike through the mangroves. I came back to work feeling refreshed and rejuvenated. Unfortunately, the calm didn't last long.

"Glad you're back, Bass," Nils said. "We need your help on a story."

As it turned out, a major story on my beat had broken while I was away enjoying the sun and surf. A local attorney had filed a lawsuit against a psychiatrist affiliated with Harvard Medical School, accusing her of causing the death of a young medical school student whom she had been treating for depression. The lawsuit, filed on behalf of the dead student's family in Texas, argued that the psychiatrist, Dr. Margaret Bean-Bayog, had had sex with the young man and reduced him to an infantilized state, eventually driving him to suicide at the age of twenty-eight. By the time I began looking in the story, the Boston news media had all but indicted the forty-six-year-old psychiatrist, and the state medical board was about to pull her license. A few of the *Globe*'s top editors had also bought into the story, even though there were very few instances of women sexually harassing men on the job.

"You know she slept with him," said Greg Moore, the deputy managing editor of the *Boston Globe*, as he passed me in the hall one day. "Here's this older woman fantasizing about a handsome young Hispanic man. You know she did it."

I didn't know that, but I knew better than to openly disagree with Greg, a smart, up and coming editor at the paper. He had made up his mind about Bean-Bayog's guilt and it seemed as though he was trying to pressure me to see it the same way.

As I worked the phones, contacting my sources in the psychiatric establishment, a very different picture of the accused psychiatrist, Margaret Bean-Bayog, emerged. It turned out that she had consulted other psychiatrists at least five times for advice on treating Paul Lozano, the Harvard Medical school student who was deeply depressed. The experts she consulted counseled her not to abandon a suicidal patient. They didn't believe she was involved sexually with Lozano. As the former head of the Boston Psychoanalytic Society told me: "What's unusual about this case—and I've been involved with many people who have been sexually abused—is that if there is abuse going on, the therapist never seeks consultation. That isn't the case here."

Bean-Bayog testified before the state medical board that Lozano was a difficult patient with a history of "horrendous childhood abuse." She said she had finally terminated her therapy with him after he refused to be supervised by the medical school committee responsible for working with impaired physicians. Nine months after she stopped working with him, Lozano died of "acute cocaine intoxication"—i.e. an overdose.

In addition to interviewing experts, I spent hours scrutinizing five hundred pages of legal filings and notes that Bean-Bayog herself had taken when Lozano was her patient. These were documents that had been turned over to the Lozano family attorney before he filed the lawsuit, and the attorney had flagged a few particularly salacious comments in an effort to prove sexual misconduct. But I appeared to be the first reporter to read all of the documents. According to Bean-Bayog's therapy notes, Lozano had discussed memories of being sexually abused by his mother when he was a young child. In the notes, there was also evidence that Bean-Bayog had fantasized about Lozano, but there was no indication that she had acted on those feelings. Instead, Bean-Bayog appeared to have dealt with her fantasies in an appropriate manner by openly discussing them in supervision and training sessions with other psychiatrists.

In the process of reporting the Bean-Bayog story, I learned how common it is for psychiatric patients to feel strong sexual feelings for their therapists and for therapists to harbor erotic feelings about their patients in return—a phenomenon known as transference and countertransference. I decided to write about this phenomenon (little-known outside the psychiatric community) and my story was published on page one of the *Boston Globe* Sunday, April 7. It was an eye-opener for many, and I received congratulatory notes from a number of readers and editors.

One day, I received a call from Ike, a well-respected literary agent in town, who said he wanted to talk to me about doing a film treatment of the Bean-Bayog story and possibly even a book.

"Jamie Lee Curtis is interested in playing Bean-Bayog," Ike said. "Can you meet with our Hollywood agent to discuss the possibilities?"

"I don't know," I said, absentmindedly twirling a lock of my hair in my fingers. "I'm not sure that's a good idea."

"You don't have to commit to anything," Ike said. "Just meet this agent and think about it. Okay?"

I felt deeply ambivalent about doing a film treatment before the full story was even known. Wouldn't that compromise my objectivity as the *Globe*'s primary reporter on the story? Even so, I agreed to meet with the agent outside a restaurant on Newbury Street in the Back Bay. We sat on a bench in the sunshine—it was in the fifties that day—but being six-and-a-half months pregnant, I was plenty warm. The agent said a Hollywood producer would pay me $5,000 just to write a two-page treatment for a film about the Bean-Bayog story. My eyes popped.

"That's a lot of change," I said. With a second child on the way, I knew the money would come in handy, particularly since I wanted to take a long maternity leave, as I had with my first baby. While the *Boston Globe* was generous with maternity leaves, allowing staff to take up to six months off for maternity leaves, the paper only covered about six weeks of that time, including earned vacation days. My husband, a social worker, and I didn't have a lot of savings, so I agreed to think about the offer.

A few days later, Muriel Cohen, a formidable reporter in her sixties whom some colleagues referred to privately as a battle axe, strode up to me.

"Can you come with me? Eileen wants to have a word with you, in private," Muriel said. I wondered why Eileen, who had worked her way up from being a secretary to a cushy job as a writer for the *Globe's* Sunday magazine, needed an emissary to talk to me. Something weird was going on. I followed Muriel out of the newsroom to the vending machines in the long corridor that led to the *Globe's* printing press. Eileen was standing in front of one of the machines; she looked nervous.

"I want you to know I've gotten an offer to do a book about the Bean-Bayog case," Eileen said. "I hope you don't mind."

I was stunned. What did Eileen know about the case? Ike had also talked about the possibility of a book contract after I did the film treatment but I hadn't made up my mind about that either. I tried to hide my surprise.

"Of course I don't mind," I said. "What's your take on this story?"

Eileen proceeded to tell me that she thought Bean-Bayog was guilty as sin and that Harvard was bringing in the big guns in an attempt to cover up for her. She implied that I was being conned by my expert sources. I badly wanted to put Eileen in her place—what, after all, did she know about psychiatry and sexual abuse—but she was not someone I wanted to cross. She had the ear of several top editors, and I did not want to get on her wrong side.

"You do what you think is right," I said. "But after poring over five hundred pages of notes, I don't think there's any evidence that Dr. Bean Bayog slept with Lozano. She may have gotten overinvolved in his case, but I don't believe she had sex with him."

Eileen's lips tightened. "We'll have to agree to disagree. Okay if I borrow the documents on the case? I'll copy them and have them back to you in an hour."

What could I say? I agreed and thanked Eileen for letting me know about the book contract. I walked heavily back to my desk, wondering just how the *Globe* was going to feel about two of its reporters writing diametrically opposed books about the Bean-Bayog case. And how was I going to write a book and have a child at the same time?

In late April, I wrote an in-depth page-one story headlined "Truth may be elusive in Bean-Bayog case," which laid out the evidence for whether or not Bean-Bayog had conformed to accepted standards of care in the psychiatry profession. The article pointed out that most cases in which psychiatrists had been found guilty of sexual misconduct involved multiple victims or one very credible victim who had a well-documented history of being harmed by sexual relations with the therapist. That wasn't the case here. Lozano was dead by his own hand, and he had left no note or other evidence blaming Bean-Bayog for his problems. And she herself had openly consulted about the Lozano case with other psychiatrists, seeking advice of other experts throughout her treatment of him.

While it appeared as though Bean-Bayog had gotten over-involved with Lozano, I didn't believe she had sex with him. It seemed as if she had done her level best to save a suicidal patient's life. But that's not what most of the media in Boston thought. Other news outlets had written thunderous editorials denouncing Bean-Bayog and calling for her resignation. At times, it felt as though I was bucking the entire news establishment.

Like other media, the *Globe*'s newsroom was divided between those who believed Bean-Bayog was guilty of sexual misconduct and those who thought she was being railroaded by an attorney and family who saw big dollar signs in a malpractice settlement. I had received several gratifyingly supportive emails from colleagues who didn't believe Bean-Bayog had had sex with Lozano or caused his suicide. One *Globe* colleague, whom I considered one of the best writers on the paper, wrote: "I have felt really proud of you and the *Globe* for resisting the easy temptation to jump on the witch-hunt bandwagon, to mix metaphors."

Yet many in the *Globe* newsroom still thought she was guilty and wanted to see her drawn and quartered. One or two of these colleagues made sarcastic comments about my reporting along the lines of, "How can you be so naïve?" Their antipathy reminded me of my own mother's longstanding distaste for psychiatrists. A good friend of hers, the mother of three young children who lived across the street from us at Bryn Gweled, had committed suicide while under a psychiatrist's care. Mom never forgave the psychiatric profession for her friend's death. I was fourteen at the time and surprised by the depth of my mom's anger and despair. Yet since then I had seen evidence of how mental health professionals could and did help in times of crisis. During my freshman year at Brandeis University, my roommate's parents both died within three weeks of each other, catapulting her into a depression. While I tried to play the clown to cheer my roommate up, it wasn't until sophomore year, after Marion had sought help from a therapist, that she finally emerged from her lethargy and began enjoying life again.

Covering the mental health beat had made me acutely aware that like any other profession, there are good eggs and bad eggs, health professionals who cared deeply about others and were willing to go the extra mile for them. And then there were those who used their power to take advantage of vulnerable patients. Any film treatment or book I wrote would probably cast Margaret Bean-Bayog as a well-meaning psychiatrist who had gotten in over her head; that, at least, was what I had concluded from my reporting thus far. But regardless of which perspective I took, I was concerned that doing a film treatment at this juncture might compromise my objectivity as a reporter still covering the story. And if I did do the film treatment or even a book, that would almost certainly put me on a collision course with Eileen. Given her powerful friends in and outside of the newsroom, Eileen was in a position to hurt my career at the *Globe* if she so chose. On the other hand, I could really use the money being dangled for the film treatment and I had always wanted to write a book. I had to make a decision soon, not least because the quandary was keeping me up at night. Which way was I going to jump?

Chapter Eight

THE DOOR TO the student newspaper office was ajar, but not wanting to be rude, I knocked anyway. "Come in," a gruff voice said.

My stomach in knots, I entered and found myself in an empty room with a beat-up black leather couch and a coffee table littered with old copies of the student newspaper, *The Justice*.

"Over here," said the voice. I swiveled around to find a stocky young man with large black glasses and a shock of sandy hair falling over his face, bent over a typewriter in a small cubicle to one side of the anteroom. It was the fall of my sophomore year at Brandeis University and I was having doubts about the wisdom of an acting career. I couldn't sing or dance (I was great at free form dancing; it was the following instructions part I was not so good at). I had also heard too many horror stories from recent graduates about having to put out for casting directors in New York. I was starting to write again—poems, a few short stories—and wondering whether there was a way I could parlay my interest in writing into something that might actually earn me a living.

The bespectacled editor detached himself from his typewriter and wandered over. I introduced myself and explained that I had an idea for the student paper. Did he have a minute?

"Whatcha got?" the editor said.

I told him I was interested in writing a regular column where I reported on the various social and cultural activities at the school with some commentary. I explained that since I was a theater major, I knew what was going on in the school's arts community. The editor, whose name I later learned was Lee, took off his glasses and rubbed them with his T-shirt, exposing a soft white belly.

"Is this something you'd be interested in?" I asked, trying to keep the quaver out of my voice.

"Maybe," Lee said. "Why don't you put something together on spec and we'll take a look? You can include activities for the next few weeks or so, but leave out the commentary. We don't have a lot of space."

When I brought in the typewritten column a few days later, it was a Sunday, deadline day for *The Justice* and the office was a beehive of activity, several students bent over typewriters, a few others sitting on the couch drinking coffee and gabbing. Lee was there as well.

He took my offering, read it quickly and grunted. "Yeah, we can use this, with some editing. Hey, you're a theater major, right? Interested in doing some theater reviews for us?"

My face flushed with nervous excitement.

"Um, okay. There's a production of *Guys and Dolls* coming up in a few weeks. I could review that."

Since I couldn't sing on key, I hadn't snagged a part in that or any of the big-number musicals being produced at Brandeis. The best part I landed thus far was a part in *The Taming of the Shrew*, which would be shown in one of the smaller theaters later that semester. I was the shrew.

As I left the newspaper office, one of the students lounging on the couch looked up at me and winked. I notice that he had a pipe in one hand and a cute baby face with dimples, but I was still so nervous that all I could manage was a quick smile as I exited the office.

That fall, I wrote several theater reviews and a monthly arts activity column for the *Justice*. I was taking five courses, and between studying and rehearsing for my part as the shrew, I didn't have time to write more or linger in the newspaper's office to chat with the other students, most of them male. But one day at the beginning of the spring semester, after I had delivered my regular column, the student with the pipe unfolded himself from the couch and came over to me. Until he stood up, I hadn't realized how tall or broad-shouldered he was. He held out his hand.

"I'm Jerry, the new news editor," he said. I shook his hand; it was warm, dry and much larger than mine. "I like your reviews. Any interest in covering some news this semester?"

Lost in Jerry's warm hazel eyes, it took me a few seconds to reply. "Um, sure. I have to get to class now. When would be a good time for me to come by and see what you have in mind?"

Each week, Jerry or another editor gave me an assignment and I endeavored to carry it out, whether it was covering a student event or interviewing the administration about a particular controversy on campus. I discovered I had a talent for interviewing people and ferreting out facts. That spring, I wrote about the origins of Brandeis (the university began as a way to combat Antisemitism in college admissions) and the spat between the administration and the faculty over salary increases. I also continued writing theater reviews. In league with my newfound interest, I switched my major from Theatre to English and American Literature, the closest I could get to Journalism (which Brandeis didn't offer as a major or a minor; it was much too practical for a liberal arts college that prided itself on being highbrow).

At some point in the spring, the collegial relationship I had with Jerry morphed into a romantic one. Jerry was even more of an outlier than I was at Brandeis, being non-Jewish and the intellectually curious son of a federal agent whose family had no idea which agency he worked for or what he really did. It's either the CIA or the NSA, Jerry whispered to me on one occasion. Jerry was about six feet tall, and he had the cutest dimples I'd ever seen. He liked wearing a worn tweed jacket with patches at the elbow, but didn't take himself too seriously. I had already lost my virginity to a much older graduate student the previous fall (my roommate Marion and I were competing to see who would be first to lose our cherries; she won). But sex with Jerry was the real deal, infused with warm, delightful feelings. That spring everything seemed brighter and more vibrant than usual, the flowers, the bird songs that woke me in the morning, the tug in my heart whenever Jerry came into view. I was in love.

Jerry and I continued our romance through the summer of 1973. We spent almost every weekend together—either down at his home on the Chesapeake Bay or in Bryn Gweled. Our time together was particularly poignant because at the beginning of September, I was heading to England for nine months. Propelled by a sense of adventure, I had decided (before I met Jerry) to do my junior year abroad. I was too lazy to learn a foreign language (as a number of my Jewish friends heading to Israel were planning to do), so England seemed a natural fit.

What better way to immerse myself in my new major than a stint in the ancestral homeland of Shakespeare and Donne? Jerry promised to visit me in England over the holidays and I have a feeling that we might have eventually ended up married if not for an incident that derailed my life and destroyed our relationship. But perhaps it was just *bashert* or destiny. Who knows?

Chapter Nine

"I HEAR YOU want in on the Watergate investigation," Ed Rademaker, my editor at *The Today's Spirit* said. A grin split his elfin face.

It was the summer between my sophomore and junior year in college and I had talked my way onto an internship at the *Spirit*, a small daily about fifteen minutes from Bryn Gweled. I was still seeing Jerry on weekends, but during the week, I needed to stay mentally keen. I finally had a job that challenged me. The summer before, between my freshman and sophomore year at college, I had worked two relatively menial jobs: from 7 am to 3 pm as a bookkeeper for 7-Eleven and as a waitress at a local pancake restaurant three or four evenings a week. At the 7-Eleven job, we were at the mercy of a tyrannical head bookkeeper with a beehive hairdo and a perpetual scowl. She routinely harangued the other women, all older than me and dependent on their jobs. For some reason, the she-witch went easy on me, possibly because I had struck up a friendship with the boss's daughter who was my age and had a summer job there as receptionist. Abby and I ate our lunches together on a bench outside the offices, soaking in the sunshine and talking about boys. Or rather we talked about her college steady and my longing for a boyfriend, or really any boy who desired me enough to stick around.

While I wasn't a bad bookkeeper (I learned some great accounting techniques that summer), I was a terrible waitress. I often mixed up the orders to the point where the cooks dreaded seeing me coming. One evening, a boisterous group of six or seven diners waved me over to their table. I had just handed them the check for their meal.

Why are you changing us extra for butter?" one man demanded. "This is ridiculous."

I shrugged. "I'm sorry sir. I have no choice. It's a directive from on high." Our boss, a harried Greek immigrant with a receding hairline, had recently instituted a policy of charging 25 cents for every extra pat of butter that customers requested. I thought it was ridiculous, given that this was a pancake restaurant and customers liked a lot of butter with their cakes.

The customer who complained stood up. He had long brown hair and was wearing a tight T-shirt that showed off his muscles. The other members of his party looked down at their plates.

"Well, you tell your boss we think it's absurd and it's coming out of your tip!" the man yelled.

I felt like throwing the plates I just cleared from the table in his face, but restrained myself.

"I'm sorry sir, I really am," I said and beat a hasty retreat.

A little while later, another customer, a middle-aged man eating by himself in one of the booths, left a $20 tip, way more than 20 percent of his bill. As I cleared the dishes from his table after he departed, I notice he had left a smiley face on his napkin. What a lovely gesture, I thought; his thoughtfulness more than made up for the rudeness of the previous customer.

When we were closing up later that evening, I told my boss what the angry customer said and how he took the extra money out of my tip.

"I don't think it's a good idea to charge extra for butter; it sends the wrong message as if we're desperate," I said.

"And who died and made you expert?" my boss retorted. "If you want to keep your job you'll do as I say!"

I gritted my teeth and nodded. As I walked away, I whispered to myself, "Only two more weeks, Ali, you can do this."

My two jobs that summer taught me a valuable lesson, that what I really wanted was a career where I would have some autonomy and never be at the beck and call of people who hated their lives and themselves. Which is why I was ecstatic over landing the *Today's Spirit* gig the summer I was about to turn twenty.

At the paper, I wrote the occasional feature and theatre review, but most of my job consisted of covering local school board and municipal meetings in the evenings (when the full-time reporters wanted off.) That meant a lot of late nights and long grueling meetings where I struggled to figure out what exactly school or city officials were talking about and whether it was newsworthy. But I had some good tutors: Ed, my editor, and Steve, an intern for the paper's parent company, Montgomery Publishing, who was a few years older than me and had considerably more journalism experience. In early August, Steve mentioned that he was driving down to Washington, D.C and suggested I come along to interview one of our local congressmen, a House Republican named Ed Biester, about the gathering political storm over Watergate.

That summer, President Nixon was being bombarded by press coverage accusing his administration of orchestrating a cover-up of the Watergate burglary. The previous fall, Nixon won re-election handily despite the fact that Woodward and Bernstein of the *Washington Post* had already published a string of stories, including the fact that the Watergate burglars were on the payroll of Nixon's reelection campaign and that a $25,000 check for Nixon's reelection campaign had been deposited in the bank account of one of the burglars. But by the summer of 1973, the media coverage had become impossible to ignore. An increasing number of Congressional representatives had even begun to talk about impeachment. Biester, a moderate Republican, was one of the few who hadn't come out for or against President Nixon.

Rademaker, an energetic, whip-thin man in his thirties with a springy light brown Afro, loved the idea of me interviewing Biester. "Try to pin him down," he said, rubbing his hands in anticipation.

When I called Biester's office to arrange an interview, his press secretary said he would check with his boss and get back to me. To my surprise, he called back in a few hours to say that the congressman had agreed to a sit-down.

In Washington, Steve dropped me off at the Capitol building and said he'd be back in an hour or two. My stomach was doing flip flops as I wandered through the ornately decorated halls looking for Congressman Biester's office. I had been to the nation's capital once before, on a road trip with my family. But I had never been inside its richly carpeted corridors of power. I felt like an imposter, an inexperienced and insignificant soldier ant who had no right to be interviewing the queen. I finally found Biester's office, and after a brief wait, was shown into his private sanctum.

Sitting behind a massive mahogany desk, Biester, who was wearing a handsomely fitted charcoal suit, smiled warmly and gestured for me to have a seat. We made some small talk and he said something nice about the *Today's Spirit*. Then I asked him about his views on Nixon and Watergate. He frowned and ignored the question. Instead, he talked about all the good things he was doing for the people of Bucks County, PA, whom he represented. I let him talk and diligently took notes. Then I asked him again about his views on Nixon and Watergate.

He glared at me and said, "I'm not talking about that today."

I looked down at my notes and took a deep breath. I knew I couldn't leave his office without getting some kind of answer. Didn't the congressman realize that Watergate was the only thing on many Americans' minds that summer? Just a few weeks prior, the Senate Watergate hearings had publicized the fact that Nixon had secretly recorded tapes of his conversations in the Oval office with Administration officials and White House staff, and the president was under growing pressure to release those tapes.

I asked Biester again what his stance on Nixon was. He stood up and started screaming at me. "Who the hell do you think you are? How dare you pester me like this!"

My mouth dropped open but somehow I remembered to jot down a few notes. That only made him angrier.

"This interview is over," he screamed. "Get of my office now!"

I was shaking when I left his office. When I met back up with Steve, he encouraged me to call my editor and tell him what happened. Ed couldn't believe what he was hearing. He had me dictate my notes to him over the phone. The result was a page one above-the-fold story the next day about how Rep. Ed Biester lost his temper when pressed by a *Today's Spirit* reporter about his views on Nixon and Watergate.

When I returned to the *Today's Spirit* and saw my byline at the very top of the news page, I had a hard time believing it. I traced the black ink with my fingers and reread the story over and over again, as if it was magic ink and would disappear on me at any moment. The sense of jubilation, of pure accomplishment, was a feeling I knew I could get used to. But as I was soon to discover, I still had a lot to learn about how to be a good journalist.

Chapter 10

IN SEPTEMBER OF 1973, I flew to England for my big adventure abroad. The nine months I spent abroad turned out to be an indelible learning experience for me, although not quite the kind I had imagined. My first week in London, I met up with Debbie L., a student from Brandeis who was bound for the University of Edinburgh, and we did the sights: the Tower of London, the British Museum, the famous department store, Harrods. We also were invited to dinner at the Hampstead home of relatives of Marion, my Brandeis roommate and best friend. There I met Brenda, one of Marion's cousins, who would end up becoming a lifelong friend. Brenda, a vivacious twenty-six-year-old, was a doer and a fixer and she helped make my year abroad considerably easier than it might have been. For starters, she knew a Londoner who attended the University of East Anglia, the same university I was headed to, and arranged to have him drive me up when the time came. Debbie left for Scotland a few days before I was slated to leave.

The day after she left, it was an uncharacteristically sunny afternoon in London. I was strolling back to the YWCA, where I had been staying. I felt great, having just had my hair cut into a fashionable page-length bob for free by trainees at the Vidal Sassoon School. Just then I heard a voice: "You ought to smile more. I bet you have a beautiful smile." I looked up; the voice belonged to a good-looking young man with jet-black hair and an engaging smile of his own. I couldn't help but smile and we chatted for a few minutes on the cobblestoned street, long enough for him to learn that I was an American just starting my junior year abroad and he was an Italian attending a London university and working part-time as a waiter.

"Hey, would you be interested in going out to dinner with me this evening?" he said. "We could go to this great little Italian restaurant that's run by a friend of mine. I think you'd like it."

I considered his offer. Truth be told, I wouldn't mind some company. The man seemed nice and polite and I figure there was no harm in going out with him in public. So I agreed to the dinner date.

That evening, the Italian picked me up outside the YWCA (no men were allowed inside) and we walked to the restaurant, which was indeed run by a friend of his. The food was delicious, and drinking Chianti by candlelight made me feel very cosmopolitan. He then suggested we go to a nearby club and I agreed. At the nightclub, we danced, drank some cocktails and smooched a little. At some point, I told my new friend that I needed to get back to the Y because I had a big day coming up tomorrow. I was getting a ride to my Norwich-based university, about three-and-a-half hours northeast of London, the next morning. We began walking back to the Y but he somehow steered me to his apartment building and asked if I want to come up for a nightcap.

"I'd like to get your contact information at school," he said. "And I'll give you mine."

I wasn't interested in another drink. "I really do need my beauty sleep. Why don't we exchange addresses here?"

He cocked his head and said in a mournful tone, "You don't trust me, do you?" Naïve idiot that I was, I went up to his apartment to show that I did indeed trust him.

Once we were inside his place, he grabbed me by the hand and pulled me into his bedroom. He ordered me to take off my clothes and when I tried to leave, he threw me onto the bed and pinned me down. I couldn't believe what was happening. He had seemed so nice, so gentlemanly just scant moments ago. Now he was a raging monster. He pulled off my clothes and when I tried to resist, he hit me. I was afraid he was going to kill me. I started sobbing and begging him to stop, but that only seemed to excite him. He raped me vaginally and then forced me to turn over. Pushing my head down into the mattress so that I could barely breathe, he sodomized me. It was very painful, something I never wanted to experience again. I concentrated on breathing, on staying alive.

When he was finally done, he told me to go to the bathroom and get cleaned up. My only thought was getting out of there alive, so when I came back from the bathroom fully dressed, I pretended everything was okay. He insisted on walking me to the Y as if nothing had happened. Once there, he asked if he could see me again. Numb inside, I said yes—anything to get him to go away. Thankfully he did, after taking down the name of my school.

The Y had already closed its doors for the night—it was around 1 am and well after curfew. I banged on the big wooden doors, praying that someone was still up. To my enormous relief, the night janitress, a matronly woman with a cockney accent, answered the door. At first she didn't want to let me in, but when I explained what had just happened, her mien softened and she beckoned me inside. She led me to a small office, made a steaming cup of tea for me, and listened patiently as I spilled my story, punctuated by desperate sobs. And then she gave me the best advice I've ever gotten. Early the next morning, she said, I should go to the nearby hospital and ask for a morning after pill, just in case the rapist had impregnated me. While such pills were not yet available in the United States or for general use in the United Kingdom, she somehow knew that London hospitals had begun stocking them for emergency situations like this.

Before turning in that night, I took a long hot shower in the women's W.C. trying to wash away my shame and horror and the stench of the rapist's body. I was furious with myself for trusting a stranger, however nice he had seemed at first. I stood under the water for a long time, letting its rhythmic drumming blot out the night's events, for a few moments at least. When I finally tumbled into my bunk, I didn't sleep more than two or three hours. Weak light seeped into the enormous barracks-like room of sleeping women before I finally nodded off.

Around eight the next morning, I stumbled out of my bunk and headed off to the hospital that the janitress told me about. My ride wasn't due until 10 am so I had time. But when I found the hospital emergency room and calmly explained what I needed and why, I was told that they didn't give out morning after pills to "loose American women" who were trying to get themselves out of trouble. I became hysterical and started sobbing that I really had been raped. Then and only then was I given the pill.

Why, you might ask, didn't I go to the police? I might have been a naïve college student from America (where my experience had been that when I said no, it meant no) but somehow, I knew that the London police would not believe me. And they almost certainly would have called my parents and that might have been the end of my year in England. I was not about to let that happen. So when I got back to the Y, after grabbing a scone somewhere, I waited for my ride. All I knew was that he was a friend of Cousin Brenda's brother; his name was Richard and Brenda had assured me he was a great guy.

During the drive up to Norwich, I didn't breathe a word about my rough night to Richard, even though he seemed kind and laid back. After all, I had just met him, I didn't know him or how discreet he was, and I was not in the mood for another lecture on how stupid and loose I was.

I think I was in shock for my first several weeks in Norwich because I didn't even write in my diary for the next seventeen days. On October 19, all I wrote was: "swimming in the black hydra of my mind; vague, watery thoughts spilling onto reflections, spotting the black hydra of my mind."

I hated myself for trusting a virtual stranger and allowing him to hurt me like this. I kept thinking I should have put up more of a fight and yet I understood deep down that I could have been seriously hurt if I had. I felt dirty, desecrated, ashamed, stupid, and bereft. The nights were the hardest when I was alone in my room and couldn't sleep. Even though I locked my door every night, the shadows played tricks on me, teasing me with doubt—was someone else in the room?—until I would get up, turn on the light, look around. No one was there, of course, and I would lie awake for hours, staring into the darkness.

It was weeks before I felt able to explain what had happened to me in letters to the people I loved most back in the States: my mother, Marion, and Jerry. And the letter writing must have helped because by late October, my diary entries were more positive, referring to the interesting personalities I'd met and how deeply stirred I was by reading Sylvia Plath's memoir, *The Bell Jar*, and her poetry. I wrote in my diary that I was "spellbound after finishing her volume [of poetry], hit with a strong, vivid, paralyzing force." Even then I was thinking of writing my own memoir about the "heavy brew of growing up."

I had the good fortune of being assigned a room on the same floor as a young English student by the name of Annie, who grew up in the Sloane Square area of London, the daughter of a wealthy art dealer. Annie was beautiful, smart, and very kind, and she was the leader of a group of co-eds at UEA whom I privately called the Sloane girls because many of them hailed from the same affluent area of London. A few days after arriving at the university, I confided in Annie about the rape and she immediately took me under her wing. Annie lost her mother to cancer when she was only twelve and I think perhaps that tragedy had made her wise beyond her years. All I know is that she was incredibly kind to me during my entire stay in England. When Annie "adopted" me, so too did her friends—not only the Sloane girls who roomed on the same floor but also her wide circle of friends in London and East Anglia. I was squired to outings and parties at various country estates in the area, where Annie's upper crust friends treated me as a curious novelty. They must have wondered what Annie saw in me—a not particularly polished middle-class American—but they accepted me into their circle because she did.

At one point that fall, Annie and her gang took me to a disco in a cavernous barn in the countryside, where we danced to loud music among people dressed in the most outlandish outfits: masks, capes, golden boots, feathers, you name it. I was amazed at the animalistic energy of my English friends once they got a little booze in them. Sober, they were reserved and unfailingly polite; goosed by alcohol, they went wild.

Annie did me another good turn as the semester wore on. I received a letter from my mother essentially blaming me for getting raped. I felt sick to my stomach with anger. How dare she blame me for something that wasn't my fault! I had already beat myself up plenty for being stupid enough to go up to my rapist's apartment with him. My father also wrote a letter berating me for what happened but he no longer had the power to wound me. Years ago, I had donned a suit of emotional armor where my dad was concerned. He had been a distant and indifferent father and I didn't much care what he thought. But my mom's response hurt me deeply. She was the parent who had always supported me, and I craved her good opinion. What I needed from her was understanding and unconditional love, not anger and blame.

Heartsick and furious, I dashed off a response saying I never wanted to speak to her again. When I told Annie what I had done, she counseled me to call my mother before she received the letter. Annie said that even though my mother was wrong, it was important for me to take the high road and forgive her. And I did exactly that, placing a brief transatlantic call (in those days, such calls were very expensive and had to be done through an operator at a pay phone in my dorm). But the phone call salvaged my relationship with my mother who apologized for what she wrote. She explained that when she was deeply hurt, she sometimes lashed out in anger.

In the phone call, she asked if I had explored the possibility of getting an abortion if I was pregnant. She said she had checked with her gynecologist who agreed to perform it if I couldn't get one in the UK.

"We will fly you home for a few days and you can fly right back," she promised. Fortunately, my next menstrual cycle was right on time thanks to the morning after pill. I also got checked for sexually transmitted diseases and came up clean.

By mid-December, I was writing in my diary that I felt safe again, sure of myself and looking forward to visits from Marion in late December and Jerry in early January. By then, I had become an editor on the University of East Anglia's student newspaper and had many British friends on campus. Indeed, at one point, another American student commented that of all the Americans at UEA that year, I was the one most accepted by the natives.

"How did you do it?" he asked with some bafflement.

I shrugged. "I don't know."

I wasn't yet willing to share the story of my rape with him and how Annie had folded me into her crowd. But even with Annie's support, it wasn't easy. I spent the first half of my year in England pining for Jerry and keeping my distance from other men (in large part because of what happened to me in London). Jerry arrived on New Year's Eve and we felt instantly comfortable with each other, falling into a relaxed intimacy as if we'd never been apart. We traveled to Edinburgh together and stayed at the house of one of my UEA classmates, the son of a Scottish lord. After a five-course meal (the main course featured venison, deer meat shot by the lord himself), the family served us Drambuie, a Scottish liquor which I loved. But storm clouds were brewing, in my mind at least. Near the end of Jerry's visit, I wrote in my diary that I was disillusioned with him, that "wonder and vibrancy no longer exist in my feelings for Jerry. All I felt is a pit of emptiness when waking next to him."

On our last day together, I accompanied him to the train that would take him to Heathrow Airport. I was in a black mood probably because of his impending departure and the thought of going back to my university alone in the middle of a cold gray winter. I also think I still hated men at this point and I wanted to lash out at a man, any man.

"I think I might want to date other people while I'm here," I blurted out.

Jerry's eyes narrowed. "I was thinking the same thing—about seeing other people."

I was stung, even though I had started this ball rolling. It was too late to stop now.

"I'm sorry but I'm having doubts. I just don't think you're dashing enough," I said, regretting the words the moment I voiced them.

Jerry's face closed in on itself. He turned away and I knew right then that I had done irreparable harm. I was right. After that visit, Jerry decided to see other women. We didn't officially break up until later that spring when Jerry embarked on a serious relationship with another Brandeis student. But my cruel and thoughtless words that bleak winter were the beginning of the end. Jerry wasn't the only man I pushed away because of being raped, but he's the one I most regret losing.

I hated being back at school. The weather was cold, although not as cold as Boston, and I remember looking out my dorm window one day at the paltry two inches of snow that barely coated the lawn, thinking that England was seriously lacking if it couldn't even whip up a storm with enough snow to go sledding or skiing on. Winter seemed to last forever, and I was counting the days until I left for Israel for my month-long spring break in April.

The moment I stepped foot in Israel I felt as if I belonged. The Israelis were my kind of people—outspoken and assertive—and while I didn't appreciate all the cutting in line at grocery stores and bus stops, I felt more at home in Tel Aviv and Jerusalem than I had ever felt in England. Even the young soldiers with their Uzis slung casually over their shoulders didn't bother me; they just made me feel safe. This was only six months after the 1973 war, which had erupted when Israel's Arab neighbors launched a surprise attack on the holiest Jewish day of the year, Yom Kippur. Even though Israel decisively defeated its adversaries, tensions were still running high when I arrived in April 1974.

Back in October when the war began, I overheard one British student saying he hoped the Arabs would drive the Jews into the sea. I was so stunned I didn't know how to respond. But that remark made me realize that some English citizens, particularly among the upper crust, were decidedly more sympathetic to the Arab cause than to a Jewish homeland, just as many of their parents had applauded Hitler's miserable treatment of the German Jews in the 1930s. Some forty years later, anti-Semitism was still alive and well in England and while I didn't hide my Jewishness at UEA, I didn't trumpet it either. In Israel, however, I felt an acute sense of belonging and pride.

I was staying with another friend from Brandeis, Debbi D., who attended Hebrew University in Jerusalem for her junior year abroad. She went out of her way to make me feel welcome and show me the sights of the old city: the western wall, the Via Dolorosa (the street where Jesus had walked with the cross), the cluttered, narrow shops that crowded the labyrinthine streets of the old quarter. I then embarked on a tour of the Sinai Peninsula. This was before Israel gave the Sinai back to Egypt as part of the historic peace agreement forged by Egypt and Israel in 1979 (which is still in place today).

Early one morning, we were roused by our guides and told we were going to climb Mount Sinai in time to see the sun rise over the historic peak where God supposedly handed Moses the 10 Commandments. It was still dark out as I stumbled out of my tent. I stood shivering in the chilly predawn, having brought only one long-sleeve shirt with me on what I thought would be a trek through a hot desert. I also had with me only one pair of shoes, a gawky pair of green suede contraptions with rubber heels. But I was determined not to let my footwear slow me down. For several hours, we followed one of the guides up a winding camel trail, over granite crags and slippery rocks. By the time, we got to the last leg of the journey—750 rocky steps to the summit—I was no longer cold. In fact, I was the fifth person in our group to make the summit (and the first female) and was able to procure a good seat on a ledge facing the sunrise. The light cast a warm glow on my face, and the rocky peaks around us turned crimson, gold, and orange. The heat of the rising sun felt glorious. As its orb climbed into the sky, the guides led us in a Hebrew prayer and we feasted on figs, matzah, and jam. I felt intensely happy and grateful to be a part of this amazing experience.

We spent the next day or two hiking into the desert to see unusual rock formations or hidden springs of water. Despite my lack of suitable gear and the endless matzah flatbread that came with every meal (it was Passover and leavened bread was forbidden), I felt alive in a way I hadn't for months.

Our tour buses slowly wound their way down the dusty peninsula to Sharm El Sheikh, then a sleepy little town at the southern tip of the Red Sea. (It has since become a major resort for Russians and Europeans, although recent terrorist attacks have hurt tourism there.) There was an amazing coral reef very close to the shore at Sharm El Sheikh, but the shallow waters that led to the reef were littered with sea urchins. That deterred many in my group from wading in, but I was determined to see the reef. Since I didn't have water shoes, I carefully floated my way out on my hands, using the salt water as ballast and keeping my eyes peeled for the tell-tale black spikes. After a few yards, the surf deepened, and I was able to swim the rest of the way. I didn't have any snorkeling gear with me and was too cheap to rent any. But I was still able to enjoy the rich assortment of beautiful fish that darted in and out of the deep reef just twenty yards from shore.

In Israel, I felt as if I had emerged from a long mental coma, a fugue state where my emotions had been numbed by despair. As I wrote to my parents after my trip to the Sinai, "I have not laughed so hard, smiled so long, had so much energy and pizzazz in months. I feel as I've come to life again … hopefully this euphoria will carry me through two more months in England." And it pretty much did.

Chapter 11

WHILE I WAS on maternity leave with my first baby, the Massachusetts Board of Medicine filed formal allegations of sexual misconduct against another prominent psychiatrist in the Boston area, Dr. Sheldon Zigelbaum. He was accused of having sex with two female patients, one of them a young woman whom he had plied with cocaine and had sex with during and outside of her therapy sessions, including once in a hot tub. Shortly after I returned from my leave in the fall of 1989, I was assigned to cover the medical board's hearing on Zigelbaum's case. One afternoon, my editor, Nils Bruzelius, walked over to my desk, a scowl writ large on his face.

"There are some folks in the newsroom who think that if we're going to mention Zigelbaum's name in the paper, we should also name his accusers," Nils said.

I stared at Nils in astonishment. It had been the policy of the *Globe*, along with other newspapers, that we didn't name victims of sexual abuse unless they wanted to be identified.

"That's ridiculous," I said. "Who's pushing this?"

Nils looked around to see if anyone else was listening. Then he leaned over my desk. "Apparently, Ziggie has some powerful friends," he whispered. "Mike Barnicle has been bending some editors' ears about this."

Barnicle was a long-time Metro columnist for the paper who fashioned himself as Boston's very own Jimmy Breslin (Breslin was a legendary columnist for the *New York Daily News*) because he too wrote mostly about working-class heroes, such as cops and firefighters out saving the world. Because Barnicle attracted a demographic that preferred reading our rival, the *Boston Herald*, he walked on water as far as top management was concerned. But his constant stereotyping—all working-class white people were good, everyone else was suspect—

irritated me, as did his swagger and general attitude of "I'm better than you are" that he seemed to project to anyone in the newsroom who wasn't a powerful white man. The news that he would be friends with a guy like Zigelbaum didn't exactly surprise me. But it made me furious and anxious at the same time. Were the *Globe*'s top editors seriously considering Barnicle's line of reasoning?

"And he's not alone," Nils continued. "From what I understand, Doris Kearns Goodwin has called some folks here as well."

My mouth dropped open in astonishment. In 1989, Goodwin was already a highly respected author; her latest book, *The Fitzgeralds and the Kennedys,* was a bestseller.

"Unbelievable," I said. "I don't understand how someone like Doris Kearns Goodwin can be friends with a man like Ziggie. Wonders never cease."

"I know," Nils said. "What do you think about all of this?"

"Well, I don't think we should change our policies on not naming sex abuse victims just because Ziggie has well-connected friends, if that's what you're asking," I said.

After my ordeal in England, I knew all too well the stigma of being known as a victim of sexual assault. I hadn't gone public about my rape, but my own parents had blamed me for the incident, as had the ER staff at the hospital in London. A few erstwhile friends whom I had told after returning to the States had also said things like, "You shouldn't have gone up to the apartment with him; what did you expect?" Or, "I'm not sure you can call it rape. After all, he wasn't exactly a stranger." After that, I learned to be very selective about who I shared my pain with. And now here it was almost twenty years later and defense lawyers for men like Zigelbaum were still trying to rip survivors' reputations to shreds in courtrooms around the country.

Nils rubbed his chin. "I agree. Don't worry, I'll push back against this."

That conversation made me more determined than ever not to miss a minute of the hearings against Sheldon Zigelbaum. At one session, the mother of one of the patients who had accused the psychiatrist of sexual misconduct, testified that Doris Kearns Goodwin, who was apparently a close friend of Zigelbaum, had called her back in 1981 and tried to talk her into not suing him for malpractice. The patient's family contacted the state medical board and sued Zigelbaum anyway and he settled the case out of court. Yet the medical board took no action on this patient's complaint until a second patient came forward to complain that Zigelbaum had sexually abused her as well. This woman did not report the abuse, which she said happened in 1986, until after I began writing about the issue of therapist sexual abuse.

I wrote a story for the next day's paper about Doris Kearns Goodwin's alleged interference in the Zigelbaum case. My story was buried inside the Metro section and the headline on the story was so innocuous that it made me laugh; it read, "Witness: Author Tried to Aid Doctor." But at least the *Globe* published the piece and after that, there was no more talk of naming sexual abuse victims without their consent. The following year, two other female patients came forward and accused Zigelbaum of sexually abusing them while they were in therapy with him, but it wasn't until early 1992 that the board finally stripped him of his medical license.

For the next two years, I continued to report on more psychiatrists who had been accused of sexual misconduct. One case in particular shocked the mental health community. Dr. Edward Daniels, a well-connected sixty-nine-year-old psychiatrist who had trained many psychoanalysts over the years and evaluated patients for referral to other shrinks stood accused by three female patients of sexual abuse. Although Daniels insisted on his innocence, he was expelled from the Boston Psychoanalytic Society in April 1990 after what its president said was a "long and careful investigation." The next week, he was suspended from the staff at McLean Hospital and placed on a leave of absence by Harvard Medical School pending an investigation by the state Board of Registration in Medicine.

That June, I wrote a perspective piece titled "the tide is turning," about how authority figures had become more likely to believe sexual abuse survivors, at least when it came to misconduct by psychiatrists and physicians in the Boston area. In that article, I noted the case of one woman who, when she first reported her psychiatrist for sexual abuse to the Massachusetts medical board, was ignored. The agency instead chose to believe the therapist, who contended that his patient was an "emotionally disturbed woman" with a serious "thought disorder."

I quoted several national experts on sexual abuse as saying there had been a remarkable change in attitude. As it turned out, their optimism was a tad premature. Anyone who watched the confirmation hearings for Clarence Thomas in September 1991 and witnessed Anita Hill being bullied and belittled by male senators from both parties could see that we still had a long way to go.

Chapter 12

BECAUSE I FINISHED college a semester early, I was able to get a head start on job hunting. After sending out fifty resumes to newspapers up and down the East Coast, I landed my first full-time reporting position with *The Easton Express* in Easton, PA (only fifty minutes from my home in Bryn Gweled). After a week of orientation in January 1974, I was assigned to the paper's satellite bureau in Flemington, N.J., which the paper had opened because it was trying to get a toehold in the relatively unsaturated Hunterdon County media market across the Delaware River. With Easton's textile mills in decay, the paper's owners knew they had to spread their wings in order to survive and the area around Flemington, home of Flemington Furs and other popular clothing outlets, was booming. Hunterdon County was even becoming a bedroom suburb for New York City, particularly for professors, actors, and literary agents who didn't need to commute into the city every day. I worked what journalists call the "graveyard shift"—4 pm until after midnight, so that I could cover city council and school board meetings, which was where the real business of local government was conducted. But I also covered crime, fires, and feature stories, and just about anything that happened on my watch after the day reporter left.

There were times, however, that I was asked to work additional hours, such as when a famous hot air balloonist came to Hunterdon County. My editor thought it would be a lark if I went up with the balloonist and wrote a feature about the experience. I was game. I had never been up in a hot air balloon before but from what I'd read, it looked like fun. Apparently, the best time to launch a hot air balloon is in the early morning hours before the wind picks up. I had to get to my office by 6 am so the publicists arranging the event could shuttle me to the take-off site, a flat meadow near the Delaware River. The balloonist, who had achieved a level of notoriety by riding a hot air balloon over the Rockies, was a slender man in his forties, with shaggy brown hair and a gap-toothed smile. I shook his hand and climbed into the basket of his huge, brightly colored red and blue balloon. He fired up the burner and yelled at his helpers to release the ropes, and with a gentle whoosh, we were air-bound. It was exhilarating. I could see the Delaware River snaking off into the distance and the distant skyscrapers of Trenton. At one point, we floated over some houses and a housewife, still in her bathrobe, waved at us from her second-floor balcony.

"I have bacon on the grill. Want to come in for breakfast?" she yelled up at us.

The balloonist yelled back, "We'll have to take a rain check, but thanks!"

We waved at her and the balloon wafted on. I was having a wonderful time until the balloonist suddenly materialized right next to me. He put a hand on my shoulder and said, "Want to play kissy face?" Oh my god, I thought, this idiot is hitting on me and I'm stuck with him in a wicker basket two thousand feet above the ground. I backed away, looking around desperately for a diversion. All I could see were some trees looming in the distance.

"Watch out," I said, pointing. "You don't want to hit those trees."

The balloonist quickly moved back to his station to fire up the burner and the balloon lifted gently, soaring over the trees. Fortunately, we were near the end of our ride, and the pilot needed to focus on landing the craft by turning off the burner and opening a valve in the fabric. He narrowly missed some more trees on our descent and our landing was bumpy. But I wasn't hurt and the minute we landed, I scrambled out of the basket. Anything to avoid playing kissy face with an overgrown man-child whose social skills hadn't progressed past kindergarten.

At age twenty-one, I was still in love with adverbs and adjectives and had trouble writing a concise sentence. So it shouldn't have come as a surprise that my editors at *The Easton Express* edited my dispatches heavily. One afternoon, I opened the courier's package from the mother ship and a copy of the article I had submitted two nights before fell out, with almost every line red-inked with edits. One of the editors, a courtly gentleman by the name of Don Henry, had slashed every adverb and adjective on the page and significantly tightened my sentences. At first I was offended—how dare he tamper with my beautiful prose? But after a few days of reading the edited copy and comparing it with my original submission, I realized Don Henry was just trying to improve my writing. And his editing helped—a lot. Now that I'm a journalism professor, I tell my students that I'm doing them the same favor when I heavily edit their assignments, just not in red ink.

One morning a few months into my new job, I got a call from my direct supervisor, a stern perfectionist who, like Don Henry, worked at the paper's headquarters in Easton. Bruce said he wanted me to cover the funeral of a young woman who had been raped and bludgeoned to death. My story about the life and death of this beautiful nineteen-year-old had appeared on page one a few days ago—my first page-one hit for the paper—and it apparently had generated a lot of interest from readers. Bruce figured the newspaper should milk the story for all it was worth. But I had a problem with that. I always thought that journalists were obligated to cover only funerals of public figures, but not invade the privacy of ordinary individuals.

"I don't think we should intrude on the family's grief," I told my editor. "I mean, her family wouldn't even talk to me." (I managed to cobble together my story about this young woman's life by talking to her friends and neighbors.)

"I understand how you feel, but I want you to go to the funeral and write about it," Bruce replied.

"No, I don't feel comfortable doing that," I said. "I just don't."

There was a long silence on the phone. Finally, Bruce said, "Alison, how much do you like your job?"

It was crystal-clear what he meant—either go to the funeral or risk being fired. Oh my God, was this going to be end of my fledgling journalism career? Was my editor serious or just bluffing? I knew deep down that I didn't want to find out. Bruce was an intimidating guy even on the phone. On the other hand, the idea of going to this young woman's funeral repulsed me; it just didn't seem right. And what if the family saw me there? They might make a scene or try to get me arrested. What was I going to do?

After a long moment of silence (I could hear Bruce breathing heavily down the line), I decided that this particular ethical dilemma was not worth losing my job over. I felt like a weasel but I agreed to cover the funeral. After I hung up, I told myself that I would be discreet. And I was. I wore a raincoat to the funeral (it was threatening rain that day, after all) and I kept my notebook in my pocket. Fortunately, there were so many other people there (curious onlookers as well as friends of the family) that no one noticed a reporter mingling among the attendees. Afterward, I interviewed a few people milling outside and wrote a passable piece for the next day's paper. It didn't make page one but that was fine with me. The fewer people who saw that I went to the funeral, the better.

By April, I had moved out of my parents' house in Bryn Gweled (spurred by the fact that my mother was charging me rent and the drive to Flemington took forty-five to fifty minutes on a good day). I found accommodations in Lambertville, New Jersey, a sleepy little town across the river from New Hope and only a fifteen- or twenty-minute drive to Flemington. My apartment was on the second floor of a private home owned by a commercial pilot and his family.

Since I worked till after midnight most nights, the drive home to Lambertville on dark, winding roads soon began to feel onerous. My plans to move to Flemington accelerated when the married commercial pilot from whom I was renting started coming onto me. He and his family lived in the ground level of the house and I lived on the smaller second floor. He made a point of bumping into me whenever I used their pool or went out for a walk around Lambertville. He even invited me up in his small three-seater plane one weekend afternoon. His oldest son, who was around ten, had come along for the ride, but that didn't stop the pilot, a sandy-haired man with an easy smile, from flirting with me as he flew the plane in and out of the clouds. When he asked me up again, I came up with an excuse not to go and started looking for another apartment in earnest.

I soon found a two-bedroom place and a roommate in Flemington itself. By this time, I had also, much to my surprise, found a fiancé.

I met Michael at a holiday dinner in Bryn Gweled the previous December, hosted by my brother Paul for his Cornell University fraternity brothers. Michael was one of the bros (like Paul he majored in engineering) and he took an immediate interest in me. We began dating long-distance—he and my brother were still in their junior year at Cornell in upstate New York—and on our first date Michael told me that he was going to marry me. I was a bit nonplussed, but being far from my Brandeis friends and working ten to twelve hours daily at a job I found overwhelming, I was lonely and grateful for Michael's attentions. What I didn't realize until later was that Michael, who was good-looking, Jewish, and very persistent, was on the emotional rebound from a relationship with a Catholic woman, whom his parents had forced him to break up with. Consequently, he was hell-bent on finding a Jewish woman more suited to their tastes. I apparently fit that bill and by late spring we were engaged.

Why, you might ask, did I accede so quickly? In retrospect (after several years of working all this out in therapy), I realized that I was still reeling from the assault in London, and emotional stability had a distinct allure. I wouldn't have to go out into the dangerous world of dating ever again. I also liked Michael's mother, a warm and charismatic woman who seemed much more empathetic and available at the time than my own mom, who was working 24/7 with my dad on getting their real estate business off the ground. One time when Michael and I visited his parents who were staying at a plush Cape Cod golfing resort on the water, I confided in his mother about the anger I felt at my mother.

"She never makes time to see me anymore," I said. "I never hear from her and when I do call her, she wants to get off the phone after five minutes. All she cares about is the business."

Michael's mother nodded sagely, all the while knitting a sleeve on a tiny green sweater. (Michael's older sister was expecting a baby in a few months and her parents were over the moon).

"It sounds like this new real estate venture is very stressful," Michael's mom said. "Give it time; your relationship will get better, I'm sure of it."

I wasn't so sure of it. So when Michael proposed, I decided it was time to make a fresh start, with a new family. I grabbed the safety net he offered, even though my own brother, who knew Michael well after several years of living with him in the same fraternity, warned me that I shouldn't marry him.

"He's not a nice guy," Paul said. But did I listen? No. Another good friend of mine who met me for drinks at a bar one weekend near Bryn Gweled, asked me why I was marrying Michael. I responded with a flippant, "Why not?"

Michael was a gifted photographer and a creative carpenter—he made beautiful furniture—but his heart was set on getting into dental school. Not because he cared about dentistry so much but because he wanted to make money and live well. He initially had set his sights on becoming a doctor but his grades at Cornell were not good enough for med school. So he settled for dental school and was accepted into Tufts University's dental program for July 1976. We were slated to be married in June and move to Boston where we would live happily ever after.

There was only one problem: I was having growing doubts about the feasibility of our relationship. Michael wasn't crazy about me being a journalist and neither were his parents, who thought journalism was not an appropriate career for a "nice Jewish girl." He was also making noises about how, once he started working as a dentist, I wouldn't need to work and could stay at home and raise children. As a feminist, I had always pictured myself as working full-time while raising a family, so I found Michael's view of domestic life jarring. He also had a tendency to criticize what I wore and would try to shush me when I got into a political debate with anyone (which I have to admit was often).

Six weeks before the wedding, I called my sister and brother-in-law in a panic. I didn't want to go through with it, I told them, I had serious doubts about marrying Michael; what should I do? My brother-in-law, Sam, counseled me to write up a list of attributes I liked about Michael and a list of those I didn't. If the negative list was longer than the positive list, I had a problem on my hands. I took his advice and sure enough the no list was longer than the yes list.

One evening about five weeks before the wedding, I confronted Michael with my doubts. He had just finished his senior year at Cornell and was visiting me in Flemington for the weekend. My roommate was away and Michael and I were sitting at the cramped dining table in my apartment kitchen.

"Sam suggested I write up a list of things I like about you and things I'm less comfortable with," I said. "And the negatives appear to outweigh the positives. I think that means we're not really suited for each other."

Michael's face turned ashen. Wedding invitations had just been mailed to more than a hundred and forty people and here I was threatening to pull out at the last moment. He stared down at his plate for a long time and then instead of getting angry, he became contrite.

"I love you, Alison, and I want to get married," he said. "I know it hasn't been an easy time with me away at school for such long stretches of time, but things will get better. I can change, I promise, I can. And I will."

I was touched by his sincerity (which may in hindsight have been desperation that I would back out at such a late date and humiliate him and his family). And I didn't really want egg on my face either. So I caved. We were married in a traditional Jewish wedding at my family's synagogue, and a week later, we moved to Boston.

Since Michael was in dental school, I was the one who had to find a job. I wasn't able to find full-time work in journalism in the Boston area, although I tried mightily. I was offered a very part-time gig as a stringer for the *Quincy Patriot Ledger*, but we needed a more stable income than that. Michael's parents, who didn't approve of journalism and wanted me to go to law school, suggested I pursue a paralegal job—to test the waters so to speak. I wasn't excited about law school, but I took their advice and landed a paralegal job with Ropes and Gray, a prestigious law firm downtown.

One morning, one of the lawyers at Ropes and Gray appeared at my cubicle waving a copy of the *Boston Phoenix*, an alternative weekly, in her hand. I had sought out some freelance opportunities once we were settled in Boston and this article was my first published effort.

"Alison, I had no idea!" exclaimed Ruth O'Brien, who, like me, worked in the firm's real estate division. She was married to a doctor, had six children, and would go on to achieve some measure of fame as the mother of Conan O'Brien.

The article Ruth was waving around concerned the opening of a new rape crisis intervention center in Cambridge. This was a brand-new concept at the time and I had interviewed both the rape crisis counselors and several rape survivors. I had not disclosed the identities of the victims because of the very real stigma attached to sexual assault.

"This is really good, Alison," said Ruth, as she plunked herself down on the edge of my desk and swung a black-booted leg. Ruth was a tall, stately woman who always wore flat-heeled black boots in the winter. "I didn't know you were interested in writing."

When I confessed my passion for journalism, Ruth encouraged me. "You'll get there," she said. "Just keep writing articles like this one."

A few weeks later, she took me home with her after work for a bridal shower she was hosting for her secretary. She lived in a beautifully appointed Victorian manse, and I remember meeting some of her children. I don't think Conan was there at the time, but if he was, he would have been thirteen years old. Ruth was the quintessential earth mother and a true role model; she showed me that women could have a career and a happy home life too.

Shortly after we moved to Boston, Michael had begun trying to transform me into his idea of a Jewish-American princess. I had never worn makeup before, so he took me to a makeup specialist in the Back Bay, who made me up to look like a hooker. I immediately washed off the paint but got the hint and started using makeup. Michael also liked taking me shopping for clothes at upscale boutique stores like Talbot's. I didn't mind the attention and the new clothes, although Michael's tastes were more conservative than mine. What bothered me was that we were spending a lot of money (which we didn't have) when I would have been perfectly happy picking deals off the rack at Filene's

Basement. At one point, we had a humongous fight over his buying me a third pair of boots.

While I was trying to navigate the shoals of marriage, my mother, at home in Bryn Gweled, decided to jump into local politics. Not only was she a long-time Democratic committeewoman, but every year until she was eighty-six, my mother volunteered as a poll worker, and rain or shine, spent Election Day welcoming people to the polls. After Stuart, my youngest brother, left for college in 1975, my mother ran for public office as a supervisor for Upper Southampton Township. She ended up winning two six-year terms and she relished her new responsibilities. Despite being the only Democrat and woman on the Republican-controlled board, she fought successfully to get a referendum passed that required the township to set aside open spaces for the community.

At some point during the contentious open space debate, I went to one of the supervisors' meetings to lend my mother support. I sat in the second row with my dad and was aghast to hear several of the other supervisors, all men and Republicans, disparaging my mom when she tried to speak up in favor of the open space referendum, which was coming up for a township-wide vote. They said she didn't know what she was talking about, that she was full of baloney and scaring people unnecessarily. I wanted to go up and smack one of the men who was being particularly insulting. He was a sleazy-looking, balding man with a pot belly and I loathed him on sight.

I turned to my father. "How do you put up with this, Dad?"

He knew exactly what I meant. "This is why I don't usually go to the meetings. I'm afraid I might punch somebody out and get arrested. And that wouldn't do your mom any good."

Much to the Republicans' chagrin, the open space referendum passed. My mother also successfully prevented a dense housing development on a hundred acres along Second Street Pike, a major thoroughfare in Southampton. Instead that property became Tamanend Park, an oasis of natural beauty amid the strip malls. Desperate to defeat my mother the third time she ran, the local Republican Party stooped to giving out flyers at area churches warning that my mother was not a Christian and should not be re-elected. She lost that election by about thirty votes and was devastated. Although she never ran for public office again, her loss was mitigated by the fact that for years afterwards, township residents would come up to her in the supermarket or at public events and thank her for what she had done for the community.

My mother's painful experience in politics only strengthened my interest in journalism. More than ever, I wanted to be one of those journalists who exposed the kind of sleazy public officials who had dragged my mother's name through the mud. I didn't yet have the experience to net a job at a major metropolitan paper like the *Boston Globe*, but I knew I needed to start making my way back toward a journalism career.

In the meantime, my marriage continued to fray. Michael was very judgmental of me—what I wore, how I played tennis. When we played doubles with his friends on a court near our apartment, he would yell at me when I missed the ball. And I was beginning to rebel against his sartorial choices. At one point that winter, he wanted to buy me a fur coat. I emphatically declined the offer. Not only could we not afford a fur coat, I told him, but I had no intention of wearing dead animals over my live body.

It took the blizzard of 1978 to fully expose the fault lines in our relationship. The city closed the roads to everyone except essential personnel and we were stuck together for a week. It didn't help that Michael, behind my back, purchased a pair of expensive cross-country skis, using money I had earned. He was thus able to venture out to ski on the empty snow-packed roads, leaving me fuming at home. When I confronted him about the purchase, he lost it.

"I want a divorce," he said. "Marrying you was a mistake."

His words shocked me. I knew we had grown apart but I couldn't believe how quickly things had come apart. I had gotten married to stay married and Michael's harsh declaration really stung. I was in shock at first and convinced he was making a mistake. In a journal entry I wrote shortly after he said he wanted a divorce, I wrote:

"I feel for him as I feel for myself. I want to reach out to him, bring him back with sympathy, show him how much I care, how much I feel until it dawns on me once more than I am the rebuffed one, the rejected alien, the one who could not measure up to his exacting standards."

As I continued to explore my feelings by writing them down, I realized that what Michael was doing, in asking for a divorce, was "for the best, the ultimate best, the twenty-years-hence best, that perhaps I could never be happy with a Michael who was so smug, so sure." By the time I had finished my journal entry, I felt as if an enormous weight had been lifted off my shoulders. I realized the marriage was beyond saving and that Michael had merely summoned the courage to put into words something we both knew to be true.

In 1978, I found a job as the health and science reporter for Harvard University's weekly paper, the *Harvard Gazette*. It wasn't strictly journalism (as a reporter for the university's own rag, I knew I wouldn't be allowed to expose any internal scandals), but I was edging closer and closer back to my dream.

At first, I loved my new job at the *Harvard Gazette*. I got to interview all sorts of eminent scientists and health-care professionals about their cutting-edge research. In the fall of 1979, two Harvard professors won the Nobel Prize for their work on quantum physics. That very afternoon, one of the newly minted Nobel laureates, Steven Weinberg, explained the theory of relativity to me using a napkin in a campus cafeteria. Weinberg articulated it so well that I was able to write somewhat intelligibly about Einstein's famous theory and how Weinberg and his colleague had confirmed a key element of it. Weinberg was not only razor-sharp and a great communicator but he was humble about what and his colleague had accomplished. Not all Harvard scientists were so nice. In my time there, I ran into some arrogant professors who thought the sun revolved around their moon and were not above yelling at a young reporter for asking what they considered stupid questions. Those experiences, while difficult, helped me develop the kind of thick skin I would need as a journalist.

Unfortunately, my boss at the Harvard News Office was also a screamer. Deane was a divorced woman in her fifties who had been born with a silver spoon in her mouth. As she was quick to tell everyone, her mother was a beautiful socialite who had once dated Clark Gable before she married first Deane's father and then a wealthy Cuban sugar plantation owner. Deane might have had great connections to Harvard's upper crust alumni, but she was widely disliked by her staff, in part because she had a predilection for publicly humiliating us at staff meetings.

One afternoon, Deane called me into her office, a huge space with room for a small conference table and piles of paper littering every conceivable surface. She stood in front of her desk, her hands on her ample hips.

"Arlie said you told him that if it looks like we're going to miss deadline, he should go ahead and start the press run without showing me the final layout," she said accusingly. "How dare you? You know I'm supposed to sign off on page one."

Shit. I should have known better than to trust Arlie, the *Gazette*'s designer. He had repeatedly complained to me about how Deane was never around to sign off on the final layout, which was why the paper's print run was often late. He said she liked to take long boozy lunches with her Harvard buddies. I merely suggested that he go ahead and authorize the press run if Deane wasn't around, to avoid missing the deadline every week. Instead, he went running to her. The weasel.

I tried to explain the actual sequence of events but Deane wasn't having it.

"I'm the boss around here, not you," she screamed. "Understand? Now get out of my office!"

I managed to make it back to my own small office before bursting into tears. And it only got worse from there. The combination of being unhappy in my job and having a delayed reaction to my failed marriage threw me into a tailspin. I began experiencing sudden crying jags at work (even when Deane was not yelling at me) and one of my friends in the office suggested I see a psychotherapist. Another friend gave me the name of a respected therapist whose office was not far from Harvard Square (apparently everyone in the news office was in therapy). I started going for weekly sessions with a clinical social worker by the name of Barbara Schwartz, a tiny white-haired woman in her sixties. Schwartz was a godsend. We delved into the effect the rape and my strained relationship with my father was having on my interactions with men.

In time, the crying jags stopped, and I gradually became less angry at my father (and men in general) and less self-destructive. My mom must have told my dad about my therapy sessions because on one of my infrequent trips home, he actually apologized to me. We were sitting across from each other in the living room one evening. My mother sat in her favorite wing chair, a silent but encouraging presence.

Dad cleared his throat and leaned forward.

"Ali, I know I haven't been a great father to you," he said. "I'm sorry about that."

I was stunned into silence. I glanced at my mother. She smiled and nodded.

"Thanks, Dad, that means a lot to me," I finally stammered.

Back at work, however, the damage had been done, and I could sense that my days at Harvard were numbered. I applied to a number of metropolitan dailies up and down the coast and somehow managed to attract the attention of editors from the *Miami Herald*. Two of them agreed to see me when they came up to Cambridge to interview Harvard students for summer internships.

The day of my interview, I walked into an office on the tenth floor of a Harvard building to find two middle-aged men there, Pete, the editor in charge of staff hiring, and Gene, a two-time Pulitzer Prize winning reporter whom I later learned had a great deal of say in the hiring process.

Pete played bad cop while Gene acted the good cop. They asked me about my journalism experience, and I must have laid it on too thick because at one point, Pete said, "If you're so good, why hasn't the *Boston Globe* snapped you up?"

I shot back, "They should!" My retort elicited an approving smile from Gene.

A few weeks later, the *Miami Herald* offered me a full-time reporting gig in one of their new *Neighbors* bureaus. I was thrilled. I had finally landed a real journalism job again and with a metropolitan newspaper that had a solid reputation for good writing. I was not sure who was happier that I was leaving Harvard—me or my boss.

Chapter 13

WHEN I FIRST arrived in Miami, a single, reasonably attractive woman in my mid-twenties, I felt as though I had a big P on my back, as in here's a woman ripe for plucking. A number of older male reporters at the *Herald* asked me out on the pretext of showing me around town, but I got the feeling that most of them were just trying to add notches to their belts. After a first date I would invariably come up with excuses for why I couldn't see them again. Even before I arrived in Miami, a friend who previously worked at the *Miami Herald*, had warned me about Gene, one of the two editors who had interviewed me for the job.

"He's a philanderer," my friend said. "Just keep that in mind if he asks you out to lunch."

Sure enough, I had only been at the paper for a few weeks when Gene, a married man in his fifties, asked me out to lunch. I didn't take him up on the offer out of fear that he might hit on me. And then what would I do? Turning him down might make him into an enemy. Gene reiterated the invitation a few months later and I came up with another excuse. I felt bad because Gene was a power broker at the newspaper and could have been a useful mentor.

After sixteen months at the paper, I was transferred to the *Herald's* Miami Beach bureau. My new beats were tourism, the Beach's lifeblood, and crime. I liked my new colleagues, especially Betty, a bubbly, blond-haired debutante who wrote features. Betty knew just about everything that was going on at the *Herald* because her boyfriend was a well-connected photographer downtown. What she told me made my hair stand on end. There seemed to be a pattern: older, married men at the paper were having sex with attractive younger women and in some cases, it appeared to be a quid pro quo: the editors were helping these women get ahead. For instance, I'd been wondering why Laura, a former Playboy bunny with no previous journalism experience, was now a reporter in the Miami Beach bureau. Betty enlightened me: Laura was sleeping with a newly minted columnist and favorite of the top brass downtown. This columnist, who happened to be married, got Laura the job, according to Betty.

Betty also informed me that my Israeli-born colleague and a friend of mine, an attractive woman in her twenties, was sleeping with the City Editor (although both were married to other people.) Betty was convinced that's why my Israeli friend had been promoted to the city desk, but I wasn't so sure. My friend may not have had good boundaries, but she was a damn fine reporter.

By then, I had heard that Gene was having an affair with a female reporter more than twenty years his junior. She was a talented writer in her own right, but some in the newsroom thought that Gene helped advance her career. (She eventually ended up at the *New York Times*). It seemed as if almost everyone at the newspaper was sleeping with someone they shouldn't be, and management didn't seem to care as long as the paper got put to bed every evening.

One afternoon, Betty and I were playing volleyball in Coconut Grove with a bunch of other pals from the paper when I became conscious of a very good-looking guy on the other team with a wicked arm. A gifted athlete, he made saves all over the net, yet when I complimented him on a great spike, he shrugged.

"Susanna set me up perfectly," he said.

Not only was this guy adorable but he was modest to boot, an unusual combination. He had curly black hair, mischievous blue eyes, and a gorgeous smile. In between sets, I introduced myself. His name was John and we flirted under the net for the rest of the game. Afterward, Susanna, who had just been named assistant editor of the Miami Beach bureau, pulled me aside and informed me that she brought John along in hopes of matching him up with Betty, who had been recently dumped by her photographer boyfriend. Susanna told me that she and her husband, who was a friend of John's from high school, were going on a double date with John and Betty after volleyball.

"I didn't realize that," I said. "Have fun!" What else could I say? Susanna was now my boss in the *Miami Beach Neighbors* and I knew Betty needed a pick-me-up.

But then a week or two later John turned up at one of our *Neighbors* softball games and pitched an amazing game. He was even better at softball than he was at volleyball. I played second base (right behind him) and we struck up a running repartee in between plays. After the game, John asked me for my number and said he would be in touch. I was thrilled. But he didn't call until the day before I was set to leave for a week-long sailing trip in the Virgin Islands with my parents and youngest brother, so our first date ended up being on New Year's Eve. Nothing like diving right in. Over dinner at a cavernous barn-style restaurant that offered dinner and a New Year's party, I asked John about Betty.

He shrugged. "I guess I'm not her type." And then he gave me that beguiling smile of his. "And she's not mine."

John was a divorced father with a three-year-old daughter on whom he doted. He had met her mother when they were both students at the University of Florida in Gainesville and they married after she became pregnant. John graduated before the baby was born, but his wife, who was a year or two younger, dropped out of school, much to his chagrin.

"She figured I was her bread ticket," he said. "She has absolutely no ambition."

John and I had a spectacular evening dancing to Motown and Rock 'n' Roll tunes spun by a local DJ. At midnight, there was a countdown and everyone started kissing each other. John leaned in and we shared an amazing kiss and that's when I knew—this guy was for real. But given my history with men, I decided to take it slow. I made it clear that my journalism job came first and that was fine with John, who also had plans. The manager of a Sherwin-Williams paint store in South Miami, he wanted to go back to school and get a master's in education. His dream was to be a school administrator.

While we spent almost every weekend together, John and I both worked long hours during the week. Having covered tourism on Miami Beach for the past eight months, I had finally figured out what the city's biggest story was: the underdog effort by one family to save the aging art deco hotels on South Beach from demolition. The spark plug behind that effort was Barbara Capitman, a former publicist and magazine editor from New York who had moved to Miami years ago. She and her son, Andrew Capitman, believed that if the art deco hotels on South Beach with their streamlined curves and nautical flourishes could be restored to their 1930s luster, they would attract a younger generation of tourists with money to burn. In 1979, Capitman had formed a group called the Miami Beach Preservation League and was able to put eight hundred art deco buildings in South Beach on the National Register of Historic Places. But city officials and a number of wealthy developers actively opposed her efforts. They wanted to demolish the aging beachfront hotels to make way for high-rise hotels and condominiums.

One day in June 1982, I met Andrew Capitman in front of the Cardozo Hotel, one of the whimsical art deco hotels that he had partially refurbished on Ocean Avenue. Even though it was already 85 degrees in the shade, Andrew, who was in his thirties, was dressed in a dapper light brown linen suit.

"Hey, thanks for coming," said Andrew. "Want an espresso?"

I declined since I'd sworn off coffee a few years ago; it gave me the jitters. Andrew showed me around inside the Cardozo, a three-story hotel painted in striking pink and purple colors. We sat down in the air-conditioned café and Andrew told me that he was struggling to raise more money from investors, especially since the Miami Beach city council had just passed an ordinance that made it difficult to preserve historic buildings.

Andrew leaned toward me. "I have a tip for you about the mayor and his real estate dealings," he whispered. Mayor Norman Ciment was one of the city's most adamant opponents of the Art Deco District. "But it can't be traced back to me."

After hearing what Andrew had to say, I raced back to the building that housed our cramped basement office. Up till now, I had not been allowed to write about the political fight over preserving Miami's art deco hotels. That was considered the province of the bureau's city hall reporter, or so my editor repeatedly informed me. But this tip about Mayor Ciment was just too good to pass up. I had to convince my editor to let me do this story.

Doug, the editor of the Miami Beach bureau, slouched behind his desk in the only office that had a door; the rest of us sat clumped together in one long narrow space behind desks almost entirely taken up by large desktop computers. Doug was a tall, reserved man only a few years older than me and I sensed that he didn't much like me. Earlier that month, he had written a negative annual review of my work, saying that I was "too opinionated and defensive about criticism," both of which were no doubt true. But I couldn't help wondering whether he would have leveled the same criticism at a male reporter. His review also said that I was a tenacious reporter and very organized, but then added [Bass] "needs to be more sensitive to others and recognize and correct her own weaknesses." His review stung, especially since I had received positive evaluations from the editors in the *Northwest Neighbors* bureau I worked in before being transferred to Miami Beach.

I explained to Doug that I had just received this great tip about a possible conflict of interest involving Miami Beach's mayor and some real estate holdings he had, which might explain why he was so opposed to the historic preservation of South Beach's art deco hotels.

"I'd really like to follow this up," I said. "That okay with you?"

Doug pursed his lips. "I think you should turn it over to Mike. He's been covering the art deco story."

"That's not fair," I retorted. "If a good tip comes to me, I should be able to follow it up myself. It's on my beat anyway."

My editor glowered at me from behind his desk.

"You know what your problem is," he said. "You don't know how to take no for an answer."

He was right. I didn't like to be told that I couldn't or shouldn't do something. My inability to take no for an answer was no doubt one of the reasons I was a good journalist. But it had landed me in hot water before. It explained why I almost got fired from my first reporting job for the *Easton Express*. I seemed to have trouble acquiescing to particular kinds of people—dour, authoritarian people like Doug and my father. And ever since the assault in London, there had been that problem of trust—trusting men, that is.

I bit my lip, trying to think of a way to persuade Doug that I was the best person to pursue this story, but before I could say anything else, he stood up, towering over me.

"Go ahead," he said shortly. "Mike is being pulled out of the bureau to work on a special project anyway. It's all yours."

Ecstatic, I began working the phones. In the span of one week, there had been a series of fires at the mostly vacant White House Hotel on South Beach's oceanfront that fire officials said were deliberately set. The final fire on July 17 succeeded in destroying the four-story hotel, which had been built in 1939 and was considered a prime example of art deco architecture. Some believed that the new owners of the hotel might be to blame—after all, they had already submitted a plan to build a 375 unit high-rise on the property and had reason to destroy the old structure. But so far no one had been arrested for arson. What Andrew Capitman told me—that the mayor had rammed through approval of the new high-rise plans shortly after his own mortgage on the White House hotel was paid off by the new owners—may have given the arsonists a sense of impunity. Perhaps they thought or had been assured that they wouldn't be punished for burning down the White House. But at this point all I had is hearsay; I had to find proof of Mayor Ciment's financial ties to the old art deco hotel. And I had a strong suspicion that wasn't going to be easy.

With the help of a well-placed source, I finally dug up records showing that Ciment and his law partners had a $376,787 mortgage on the White House Hotel and that the hotel's new owners, Indeco Holdings, paid off the entire mortgage weeks before city officials approved their plan to build a thirty-seven story, 375 unit condominium building on the ocean-side site of the White House. (The payoff still had not been recorded in the Miami-Dade County office, as required by law.) The new luxury condos were to be called Place Mishal, because one of the principal backers was Saudi Prince Mishal Bin Saud. And then of course, the White House burned to the ground a few months later in a fire that officials strongly suspected was arson. The paper ran my story about the mayor's paid-off mortgage inside its Metro section, and I got a note from the investigations editor downtown: "Nice job

Bass! Keep up the good work." (As it turned out, Indeco's thirty-seven-story monstrosity was never built; the company defaulted on its loan and the bank sold the property to another builder with more tasteful plans for the oceanfront site).

In early August, John and I left to take a long-planned week-long vacation with my family on the Vineyard. We were having a wonderful time until I got a phone call from someone in the *Miami Herald's* Human Resources Department. I was being transferred to a *Neighbors* bureau in West Broward County. My new job meant that I would have to commute almost an hour to work each way if I wanted to continue living in Miami. I was beside myself. Why was the paper punishing me like this? Was it because some influential politicians didn't like the stories I was writing? Or was it because I had flouted my editor's directive about not writing stories about local city officials? I supposed it didn't really matter why. I was being sent to the newspaper's version of the boonies and there was nothing I could do about it. Except walk.

A week after I returned from vacation, I started my new gig in West Broward County, traveling forty miles each way. I also began looking for another job, even though I was reluctant to leave South Florida. At this point, John and I had been together for about eight months and I was in love. Shortly after getting back from the Cape, we had had a heart to heart talk and John encouraged me to find another job, promising to come with me if I landed something outside of Florida. I was moved by his declaration and enormously relieved. But deep down I didn't believe him. I doubted that he would ever leave his daughter.

In my new posting, I was assigned to cover Margate, a once-sleepy little town in West Broward County that was experiencing an influx of retirees who had fled the cold winters up north. Snowbirds we called them. One evening, I was attending my second meeting of the Margate City Commission, which had been droning on for at least two hours. It was past 9 pm and I was struggling to stay awake and figure out what's going on. Just as I stifled a yawn, Abe, one of the elected commissioners, a gaunt retiree wearing a loud Hawaiian shirt, picked up a piece of paper in front of him and squinted at it. He looked at Tom Hissom, the city manager who sat at a desk to the side of the commissioners' elevated console.

"Are we still negotiating for the sale of our water and sewer system with the county?" Abe asked. "I thought I heard it wasn't going to happen."

Hissom sighed and I noticed that he studiously avoided looking at the man sitting next to him: Doug Darden, the president of Envisors, an engineering firm contracted by the town to appraise an aging sewer and water system that Margate owned in nearby Collier City and negotiate its sale to Broward County.

"You're right, Abe," Hissom said. "The county is no longer interested in purchasing the water and sewer system."

Abe frowned. Even though this was only the second commission meeting I'd covered since being transferred to West Broward, I'd already pegged Abe as an independent type, one of the only commissioners who didn't automatically fall in line with the power brokers on the commission.

"Well, then, why are we paying Envisors $6,000 for negotiations on the sale, if there isn't going to be a sale?" Abe demanded. "That's a hefty chunk of change."

Hissom glanced at Darden. "You want to explain this one?"

Darden, who was wearing an expensive-looking pinstripe suit, exchanged a freighted look with Jack Tobin, who wielded a lot of authority on the commission. Tobin was a short, plump man who, like Darden, dressed as if he belonged on Wall Street, not a stuffy meeting room in Nowheresville, Florida. Tobin was a man on the rise; he was running for a seat on the Florida state legislature that fall, and most of the other commissioners seemed in awe of him.

"We did a lot of work to prepare for the sale even though it fell through," Darden said. "Anything we do in excess of the [appraisal] report, I bill the city for."

Tobin inclined his head approvingly. "I think we should pay this invoice. Doug's team has worked very hard on this deal and they deserve to get paid. It's not his fault the county reneged."

Two other commissioners nodded in agreement. Abe tossed the invoice back onto the table, but said nothing more. A while later, the commission passed a motion to pay a bunch of bills, which included the invoice Abe questioned. The meeting finally adjourned shortly after 10 pm. As I stumbled out of the chambers, thanking my lucky stars I didn't have to file a story that night (we were on a bi-weekly deadline), I resolved to ask some questions of my own.

The next day, I walked into Margate City Hall and asked to see the city manager. The secretary informed me that he was out, but I could talk to the deputy city manager if I wanted to. I did. The deputy city manager was a friendly young man who seemed happy to see me. When I explained that I'd like to talk to him about the Envisors' invoice discussed at last night's meeting, he beckoned me to sit down in a chair in front of his desk.

"I'm glad you're asking about this," he said. "But this has got to be off the record. You understand why."

I did. The deputy city manager could lose his job if word got out he was talking to the press.

"Of course," I said. "But do you mind if I take notes just for myself? I promise I won't use your name in the paper."

The deputy city manager explained that the city of Margate had been paying Envisors an exorbitant sum of money to appraise a water and sewer system it owned in nearby Collier City for sale to the county.

"The commissioners approved a $47,000 contract to Envisors for the appraisal and sale negotiations two years ago," the deputy manager said. "Of that amount, $35,000 was to appraise the system and $12,000 was to conduct sale negotiations with the county. But the county changed its mind and there haven't been any negotiations. Yet we ended up paying Envisors even more than the contract called for."

I looked up from my notebook. "Are you saying Envisors is billing the city for work they never did?"

My source looked me in the eye. "Yes, that's what I'm saying. And that's not all."

He explained that both the county and Pompano Beach, a city that had been planning to hook into the Collier City system and do the needed repairs on it, had each only spent $10,000 to appraise the system.

"So why is Margate paying more?" I asked.

"I'll get to that," he said. "But there's more."

Last year, he said, the city commissioners agreed to pay Envisors an additional $275,000 for a study of Margate's entire water and sewer system, despite the city manager's vehement objections that the amount was too high.

"Tom told the commission that the study could have been done for as little as $50,000, but they went ahead and approved the contract with Envisors anyway."

"Why?" I asked again.

The deputy manager leaned toward me and whispered, "I think there's money changing hands, but we have no proof of that."

Wow, I thought. This was a great story, even if I couldn't nail down the bribery angle. The allegations didn't surprise me though. In my twenty-nine months of working for the *Miami Herald*, I had noticed that corruption seemed to be rife, particularly in the once-quiet hollows of Dade and Broward counties that were experiencing a growth spurt as retired snowbirds and tourists flocked to southern Florida in search of balmy weather and velvet sands.

"Can I see the documents showing the amount the town has paid Envisors?" I asked. "And how can I prove that there's been no negotiations on the proposed sale?"

The deputy city manager nodded. "I'll ask Margie to collect the invoices for you—it's all a matter of public record. She'll probably even make copies for you. And you can call John Kelly, the project coordinator for the Broward County Community Development Division—he'll tell you there were no sale negotiations."

The deputy city manager also gave me the name of a city official in Pompano Beach who could confirm how much that municipality paid to appraise Collier City system.

Sure enough, when I returned the next day, copies of the paid invoices to Envisors over the last two years were all stacked neatly on the secretary's desk; she herself was off to lunch. I saw that the city had paid Envisors a total of $52,571 for its work on the Collier City contract. I also noticed the engineering firm charged Margate $180 an hour for its word-processing services, which seemed a bit steep to me. When I got back to the bureau, I put a call in to John Kelly and the Pompano Beach official. Then I told Doug Delp, my new editor, about the developing story.

"You've got a live one here, Alison," Delp said. "Good job." Delp was a crusty Vietnam vet who didn't seem threatened by my zeal for digging into controversial stories. He was as different from Miami Beach Doug as night and day. He took me off another assignment so I could finish reporting out the Margate story.

The next day, I reached John Kelly and he confirmed there had been no negotiations on the sale of the Collier City sewage and water system. The Pompano Beach official also called back and put me in touch with the engineers who did that city's appraisal of the system and the county's appraisal. The engineers for both Pompano Beach and Broward County said that Margate overpaid Envisors for the Collier City negotiations and for the study of the sewage and water system the contracting firm did the previous year. They also noted that the county and Pompano Beach went through a competitive bidding process to select their engineering consultants, while Margate did not. And finally, they told me that most consultants charge between $16 and $22 an hour for word-processing services, not the $180 an hour Envisors charged Margate.

The deputy city manager confirmed that Margate officials had avoided competitive bidding by making the Collier City contract a "supplement" to their separate contract with Envisors to work on the city's wastewater plant expansion. Since 1980, the city had paid Envisors more than $1.3 million in engineering fees.

My next phone call was to Margate's city attorney who told me that the supplemental contract was perfectly legal. I also called several of the commissioners who voted to approve the various contracts with Envisors. Tobin never returned my phone call but I finally reached Richard Schwartz who said he thought the payments were more than reasonable.

My last phone call was to Doug Darden, the president of Envisors. He says the $52,517 paid for the Collier City work was justified because his firm did far more work than Pompano Beach's consultant. "You get what you paid for," he said.

And why did he bill the city for sale negotiations that never took place? He said that was because it took his firm more than $35,000 in labor and time to prepare the appraisal report. "Anything we do in excess of that, I'll bill them for," he said.

The deputy city manager had already shown me the minutes of a meeting in 1980 when Darden promised city officials that if the sale fell through, they wouldn't be billed the $12,000 for negotiations. Darden had nothing to say about that. When I asked why his firm charged the city $180 an hour for word-processing services, he replied, "It beats the hell out of me." A minute later, he added, "We pay mucho bucks for word-processing because we have a top-of-the-line word processing system."

On October 24, 1982, the *Miami Herald* published my story: "Margate paid $6,000 for job never done, county says." I followed up with another story about the cozy relationship between Doug Darden and several of Margate's city commissioners. Several top editors wrote me congratulatory notes. But the accolades came too late. I had started looking for another job as soon as I was transferred to the West Broward boonies and by the end of October I had been offered a job with *Technology Review*, a science and technology policy magazine published by MIT in Cambridge, Massachusetts.

Doug Delp tried to talk me out of leaving.

"There's more to this story Alison and we need you on it," he said gruffly

I was tempted; it would be nice to nail down the rumors of bribery and kickbacks. But I'd had it up to here with the *Miami Herald* and being called "honey" by men wearing white shoes. Newspaper journalism, at least as practiced in Miami, was no different than the surrounding milieu, which was ripe with cronyism and a "if you scratch my back, I'll scratch yours" mentality. The white men in control of the *Herald* were simply more comfortable with guys who looked and acted like them (and could talk football with panache) or with young women they could seduce. They had no idea what to do with a female reporter who was aggressive and outspoken, "a brassy northern broad," as one friend of mine put it with just a touch of irony. (After I left the paper, other *Herald* reporters picked up the trail in Margate, which eventually led to the indictments of two former Margate officials, including Jack Tobin, who had been elected to the Florida legislature that November. Tobin and former Margate Mayor George Liederman were charged with taking money from Envisors in return for awarding them the lucrative engineering contract; Darden was also indicted. When the indictments were announced, Doug Delp mailed me a packet of news clips with a letter saying, "Seeing as how you started all this, I figured you might be interested in the enclosed.")

In 1984, the same year the Margate indictments came down, the Capitmans, having run out of money to refurbish their art deco hotels, sold the properties at a loss to another company. Andrew left Miami and eventually became a hedge fund manager in New York, and his mother died in 1990. But other developers took up the fight to save and restore the art deco district and by the 1990s, South Beach had become what one writer called "America's Riviera," a striking oasis of beautifully restored hotels that attracted celebrities, models, and upscale tourists from around the world. Barbara Capitman's vision had exceeded even her own far-sighted expectations.

But who could have foreseen all of this in the fall of 1982? Even though Delp and I got along great, I didn't want to stay in a job where I had to commute almost two hours every day. I tried to negotiate with the managing editor for a gig back in Miami covering health, but he made it clear that wasn't going to happen any time soon. So I decided to accept the MIT job. My only regret was leaving John. Even though he promised to come with me, at the last moment he changed his mind. He just couldn't leave his three-year-old daughter. I was heartbroken but not surprised. Deep down I had known it would come to this, which was why I had stuck it out in Miami for so long.

I sold my Honda Civic and any furniture that I could unload, bundled up my two cats in crates, and said a tearful goodbye to John at Miami International Airport. We agreed to attempt a long-distance relationship but I knew how tough that would be and wasn't feeling optimistic.

On my way to Boston, I stopped for a few days in Bryn Gweled to spend Thanksgiving with my family. I took long walks on the trails that wound through the woods around the homestead. The crisp air and rustling leaves underfoot soothed my soul and helped me prepare for a life without John. Surrounded by a boisterous family and the gentle rolling hills of my childhood, I began to look forward to a future that accepted me for who I was, a brassy northern broad who couldn't help stepping on toes in my pursuit of the truth.

Chapter 14

IN JANUARY OF 1990, I was heartened to learn that the *Globe* planned to nominate my series on sexual abuse by psychiatrists for a Pulitzer Prize in public service. My editors nominated the series in part because no one else in the U.S. had written in such a systematic way about the sexual abuse of patients by male professionals in positions of power over them. This was, after all, twenty-eight years before the #MeToo movement, and rampant sexual exploitation of vulnerable women was not talked about, much less written about. I had broken some taboos in writing about this subject, and one top editor told me I was a rising star at the paper. But the series didn't win. The public service award went to the *Des Moines Register*, which had published a five-part series about an Iowa woman who decided to go on the record with the detailed story of her rape. In those days, the stigma against sexual assault victims was even harsher than it is today, so most reporters didn't identify victims as a matter of course. *The Register's* series sparked a national debate about that policy and prompted most newspapers to identify victims, but only if they consented.

In August of 1990, the American Psychological Association held its annual conference in Boston and I obtained an advance copy of the program. One particular abstract jumped out at me as I pored over the program at my cluttered desk in the newsroom, an expansive sea of desks illuminated by windows on three sides and overhead fluorescent lighting. The abstract alluded to a twenty-five-year study done of U.S. priests' sexual practices by A.W. Richard Sipe, a former priest who was now a sociologist at Johns Hopkins University in Baltimore. After surveying a thousand priests, Sipe concluded that a surprisingly high percentage of priests in the U.S. were not celibate and that the Catholic Church's insistence on celibacy was seriously eroding its credibility on matters involving human sexuality. Sipe's findings were newsworthy given that a

Catholic priest who founded the Covenant House, a halfway house for runaway teens in New York, had recently resigned after reports that he had sexually abused a number of homeless adolescents who sought help from the Covenant House. And just the previous month, the nation's first black archbishop had resigned his post in Atlanta after reports that he had a sexual relationship with a female lay minister.

The next day, I attended Richard Sipe's talk, which was held in a small, nondescript conference room at the Prudential convention center. I was pleased to see that I was the only journalist in the room. I was able to interview Sipe briefly after his talk as well as one or two other sociologists who attended the session. I then raced back to my office, where, after briefing my editor on what I had, I put in a call to a spokesman for the US Catholic Bishops and started writing my story.

I knew the story would be explosive, not only because Sipe had found that only forty-six to forty-eight percent of priests in his study actually practiced celibacy, but also because, based on the priests' own accounts, six percent of those in his study had molested children or adolescents. I was right. Once I filed the story and Nils had edited it, other editors weighed in, essentially trying to water the story down. They moved up the response from the Church attacking the credibility of Sipe's research to the top of the story and moved down to near the end the shocking statistic about how many priests said they were sexually involved with children and adolescents.

Even then, there was a contentious debate among the paper's top editors about whether to put my story on page one or bury it in the Metro section. Several editors felt the piece was disrespectful to the Catholic Church and would ignite a backlash against the paper. After hearing everyone out, Helen Donovan, then managing editor of the *Globe* who made the final page one calls, decided it was page one material and there the story ran on August 12, 1990. Nils told me later there had been some grumbling about the story, particularly from one of the top editors, a Catholic, who felt the story was biased and shouldn't have been published on page one. A number of my colleagues congratulated me on the scoop, but I was not encouraged to follow up and write anything more about Sipe's research or Catholic priests who violate their vows.

The *Globe* published nothing more on this topic until May 1992 when attorney Eric MacLeish called me late that afternoon to tell me he was representing nine men and women who had accused a former Roman Catholic priest of molesting them when they were children living in southeastern Massachusetts. My first Father Porter story ran on May 8 and on May 12, I broke the news that thirty additional victims had come forward to charge Porter with molestation when they were children in the 1960s. The following day, I wrote about a little-known law in Massachusetts that limited the Church's liability in sexual misconduct cases to $20,000.

Other Metro reporters weighed in and on May 24, Cardinal Law, the titular head of the Boston Archdiocese, called down the wrath of God on the *Globe*. Despite Law's threats, the newspaper did not back down. Indeed, under Metro Editor Ben Bradlee's direction, the paper started ramping up its coverage and investigated the Church's handling of Father Porter who had been moved around from parish to parish in the Archdiocese. By the end of May, Bradlee decided to take me off the story and put it in the hands of two seasoned Metro reporters who were prepared to travel and dig into the Church's culpability in the Father Porter case. I have to admit I didn't put up much of a fight. More than seven months pregnant by then and huge with a baby that promised to be even larger than my first one, I was secretly relieved to be off of the Father Porter narrative. At that particular point in my life, I just didn't have the energy to travel and spend countless hours digging into this contentious story.

From then on, most of the bylines on that story were owned by two Metro reporters, Linda Matchan, and Stephen Kurkjian. In June, Linda wrote a hard-hitting piece about how church officials knew about the sexual misconduct complaints against Father Porter while he was at St. Mary's school. But instead of taking action, Church officials transferred him to Sacred Heart Church in Fall River, where he was allowed to supervise altar boys and other children. He was transferred again in 1965 to St. James Church in New Bedford, where he remained until

1967 when he left Massachusetts. Linda and Steve even traveled to New Mexico to scope out the treatment center that Porter and other priests were sent to for treatment after being accused of sexual molestation. They discovered that while Porter was being treated at the New Mexico center for pedophilia (currently defined as a psychiatric disorder in which an adult fantasizes about or engages in sex with prepubescent children), Church officials allowed the priest to serve in several nearby parishes where he molested a dozen other boys.

In December, the Boston Archdiocese announced it would settle with about sixty-eight alleged victims of Father Porter for at least $5 million if they would drop their lawsuit against the Church. A settlement was reached, but more victims of Porter and other priests kept coming forward so our coverage didn't stop there. One story in late March 1993 revealed how one of the delegates named by Cardinal Law to investigate sexual abuse complaints in the Church had not acted on a complaint against a Boston priest made directly to him in 1985. In interviews with a *Globe* reporter, David Coleman, age forty-five, of Eastham, said that he had informed Rev. John McCormack, one of the delegates later appointed by Law to handle sexual abuse complaints, of being molested by this other Boston priest numerous times over a four-year period beginning in 1958, when Coleman was nine years old. But McCormack took no action against the offending priest and years later the same priest was accused of sexually abusing boys in a California choir. The March 31 article also noted that more than a hundred persons in Massachusetts and several other states had come forward to accuse Father Porter of sexually abusing them while he was a priest.

The same month, Matt Storin, a respected journalist who had worked at the *Globe* in the seventies and early eighties, was named the paper's new editor in chief. A few months later, Storin, who was Catholic, issued an edict: No more Father Porter stories. There was no explanation for Storin's order, but according to the general scuttlebutt in the newsroom, he was finally bowing to pressure from the Church. Unbeknownst to Storin, however, there was one more story in the pipeline: a long piece for the *Globe* magazine by Linda Matchan about how the small town of North Attleborough had harbored the secret of Father Porter's proclivities for young boys behind a "town-wide institutional denial." Mothers who knew that the priest had fondled their sons were told that no one would believe them if they came forward. As Linda eloquently wrote, this was "before the days of Oprah, a more trusting and innocent period when words like 'pedophile' and 'sexual molestation' were not part of most vocabularies, when the actions of Catholic priests were not questioned, the judgment of their superiors never second-guessed."

When Matchan's piece was published on August 29, Storin hit the roof. He charged into the magazine editor's office and screamed at her at the top of his lungs, yelling that her career at the *Globe* was over, that she was persona non grata from that point on. I heard about his meltdown from a graphic designer who had witnessed it. I was shocked by Storin's tantrum and felt sorry for the magazine editor who bore the brunt of his rage. I have to admit I was also secretly relieved I was no longer on the Father Porter story.

After Storin's edict, our stories about errant Catholic priests pretty much petered out, with a very occasional story that we simply couldn't ignore, such as when Eric MacLeish, the lawyer who had helped break the first Father Porter story, gave the *Globe* another explosive tip: he had forwarded child abuse accusations to Boston archdiocese officials involving twenty other Boston area priests. MacLeish said the archdiocese had put all of these priests on indefinite leave but because the Massachusetts statute of limitations for charging them with criminal conduct had expired, nothing else could be done. This story should have made page one, but instead it was buried inside the Metro section. Worse, there was no attempt by *Globe* reporters to investigate what looked like a systematic and widespread cover-up by the Church. The only other stories that ran in the *Globe* after Storin's edict were about Father Porter being found guilty of multiple counts of sexual abuse and sentenced to eighteen to twenty years in prison. (Porter later died in prison in Minnesota, where he settled after leaving Massachusetts.)

The ban on digging into the Church's role in covering up clerical sexual abuse lasted until Storin was fired in 2001. He soon landed a cushy PR job at the Catholic-run University of Notre Dame. Was this a quid pro quo for his actions in protecting the Church while he was editor of the *Globe*? To those of us who had worked at the paper during this tempestuous time, it sure looked like it.

Storin was replaced by Marty Baron, a highly respected journalist who had worked for the *New York Times* and other newspapers. Marty was Jewish and new to the Boston area. As the 2016 movie *Spotlight* makes abundantly clear, one of Baron's first acts as executive editor was to direct the Spotlight team to look into how the Boston Archdiocese had handled the ongoing problem of priests sexually abusing altar boys and other children in their parishes. The editor of the Spotlight team at the time was none other than Walter Robinson. Robby, as he was known in the newsroom, had been Metro Editor under Storin when the story about the sexual abuse accusations against twenty other priests in the Archdiocese was buried in the Metro section.

A politically savvy Vietnam vet with well-honed investigative skills, Robby had been the *Globe*'s Washington bureau chief in the early nineties and had steadily moved up the ladder under Storin. But now there was a new sheriff in town and Robby did what he was told. He led the Spotlight team's investigation into how the Boston Archdiocese had handled the case of yet another priest, Father Geoghan, who stood accused of sexually molesting young boys in a half-dozen parishes in the Boston area. In 2002, the *Globe* published its damning series on how the Boston Archdiocese had covered up horrific tales of abuse by Geoghan and other priests through an elaborate system of secrecy and intimidation. Victims who came forward with abuse claims were ignored or paid off, while accused priests were quietly transferred from parish to parish or sent for brief periods of psychological counseling. After the *Globe*'s eight- part series was published, Cardinal Law was forced to step down and the Spotlight team's work won the Pulitzer for public service the following year.

More than a decade later, the Oscar-winning movie *Spotlight* dramatized the paper's efforts. As I wrote in the *Huffington Post* in early 2016:

Spotlight is a riveting movie that gets a lot right . . . But there are a few things the film doesn't get quite right. The biggest disappointment is the way it glossed over the reporting that had been done by *Globe* writers about the priest scandal well before the Spotlight team sprang into action in 2001.

The movie also made it sound as though the *Globe* Spotlight team was the first to discover Richard Sipe's landmark research on priests' sexual proclivities. The film made a big deal out of this discovery, which I found rather funny, because all the Spotlight team had to do was search their own archives, where they would have found my 1990 story.

Chapter 15

I HAD A big decision hanging over my head. I still hadn't made up my mind as to whether I should do the five-page treatment for a movie about Margaret Bean-Bayog or accept one of the book offers that my agent was dangling in front of me. I remained the primary reporter on the Bean-Bayog story and I worried that writing a film treatment might compromise my journalistic integrity. From everything I had dug up so far, it looked like Margaret Bean-Bayog was getting railroaded by the malpractice attorney who represented the family of Paul Lozano, the medical student who committed suicide nine months after she stopped treating him. While other members of the press, including some in the *Globe* newsroom, were convinced that Bean-Bayog had seduced Lozano and was responsible for his death, I had found no evidence of that.

When the Bean-Bayog story was thrown into my lap at the beginning of April 1992, I read all the documents that were part of the court records in the ongoing malpractice suit against Margaret Bean-Bayog. Some of these documents were revelatory to say the least. According to medical records obtained from several psychiatrists who had treated Lozano at McLean Hospital, a psychiatric hospital in the Boston area, years before he sought help from Bean-Bayog, Lozano had admitted to being severely abused as a child and had attempted to commit suicide numerous times before. On my first day back from vacation, I wanted to delve deeper into these records, but I was facing a tight deadline and had to start writing for the next day's paper. In the meantime, the reporter who had filled in for me drew my attention to a new filing in the case. A social worker who treated Lozano had filed a court affidavit that day alleging that he had no psychiatric problems before being treated by Bean-Bayog. The social worker stated that Lozano also told her that he was having a sexual relationship with Bean-Bayog. So that became the lead for my first story published April 2. I included a statement from Bean-Bayog, calling the social worker's claims about Lozano inaccurate. As I was soon to find out, she was right. In that initial story, I also included what I'd seen in the medical records about Lozano's suicidal attempts prior to meeting Bean-Bayog.

The next day, I continued plowing my way through the five hundred pages of documents that had been filed in the court case thus far. My story for the April 4 newspaper broke the news that Lozano had been diagnosed by at least four psychiatrists as suffering from borderline personality disorder—a disorder characterized by impulsive, manipulative, self-destructive, and suicidal behavior. People with border personality disorder often lie to manipulate others around them, a fact I thought had bearing on this case.

I followed that up with my page one story on April 7 about how common it is for psychiatric patients to feel strong sexual feelings for their therapists and for therapists to harbor erotic feelings about their patients in return.

By then, I had discovered something else of note in the medical records. The very social worker who had earlier filed an affidavit saying that Lozano had no psychiatric problems before being treated by Bean-Bayog had herself written in the McLean Hospital records that Lozano did have a history of depression and had been abused as a child. That became the lede of my April 9 story:

> A social worker who filed an affidavit in court last week saying that Paul Lozano had no history of psychiatric problems before being treated by Dr. Margaret Bean-Bayog acknowledged yesterday that she had written in his medical records that Lozano had a history of depression and had been abused as a child.
>
> While she was a social work intern at McLean Hospital in September 1986, Amy Stromsten wrote in Lozano's medical records that "there were many incidents of abuse in Paul's childhood" and that he "is very estranged from his family."

She further noted that Lozano's roommate had told her that "Paul suffered from seasonal depressions" and had gone "downhill" after a car accident in January 1986. That was six months before Lozano began therapy with Bean-Bayog, the psychiatrist whom Lozano's family had accused of sexually abusing him and causing him to commit suicide.

A few weeks later, I broke the news that a retired Fenway electrician filed an affidavit in the case saying that he had saved Paul Lozano from killing himself in the spring of 1986, several months before Bean-Bayog began treating him. A few days later, I wrote a more in-depth piece about how if the allegations of sexual misconduct against Bean-Bayog were not proven (and it looked increasingly likely they wouldn't be), the case against her boiled down to the murky issue of whether she had conformed to accepted standards of care in her profession.

By this time, I had made my decision. Since I was still covering the Bean-Bayog story, I decided not to write a film treatment or pursue a book contract. The Metro Editor scoffed at me for turning these opportunities down. "You're a fool," Ben Bradlee Jr. said. "Everybody does it now."

But I felt deeply uncomfortable about writing a film treatment that would no doubt depict Bean-Bayog as a well-meaning psychiatrist who had gotten in over her head (which is what I believed), while I was still on the beat. And I knew I couldn't write a book; I had a baby coming in three months and I wouldn't have time to churn out a book on deadline while caring for a newborn. I turned both the film and book opportunities over to a freelance writer who had been helping me with the Bean-Bayog coverage. I had to admit that I was secretly relieved not to be going head-to-head with Eileen, the reporter who had already gotten a book contract to write about Bean-Bayog and who firmly believed she was guilty.

In mid-July that year, I wrote one more story about Margaret Bean-Bayog, relating how her attorneys were outraged that the state medical board had decided to postpone her July hearing and seek the help of outside counsel, a highly unusual move. The hearing was rescheduled for Sept. 1 and state officials decided to move it to a much larger venue in another government building to accommodate the expected media crowd. Writers from national magazines like *Vanity Fair* and *People* were planning to parachute in and it promised to be a zoo. Since my son was due in mid-August, I would be on maternity leave by then— much to my relief.

I started my maternity leave the second week of August and my son, Jake, was born on August 19 by cesarean section. It took me six weeks to recover from the surgery and after developing a breast infection, I reluctantly had to stop breastfeeding and turn to feeding him with a bottle. We had moved to a three-bedroom, two-story house in Newton, Massachusetts the year before, and I was inordinately grateful that my mom once again came up to help out, since I was not allowed to go downstairs until my stitches healed. She took my son, David, to his preschool every morning and cooked dinner for us every night until I was able to get downstairs again.

As sleep deprived as I was, with early morning feedings and taking care of two children under the age of four, I still found time to read the *Globe* every morning. I saw that Dr. Bean-Bayog had resigned her medical license in late August to avoid what her lawyers said would be a "media circus" at her hearing. In December, she settled with the Lozano family for $1 million (with no admission of liability) and disappeared from the spotlight.

In the meantime, I was exceedingly busy trying to juggle motherhood and a demanding career. Lucky for me, after I returned from my second maternity leave in January of 1993, the *Globe* allowed me to work a four-day-a-week schedule, pro-rating my pay and benefits for a year or two. I was also fortunate to be married to a man who was very invested in being a father and whose social work job allowed him to leave work at a decent hour, collect our boys from day care, and get them home in time to cobble together dinner. I would get the boys up the morning, drive them to day care or walk them to school, and then go to work. It was an exhausting, if exhilarating, time for me, and while I often felt guilty that I wasn't spending enough time with my two young sons, I felt lucky that I had a job that challenged me and that I loved, most of the time anyway.

The two books about the Bean-Bayog case by Eileen and Gary, the freelancer, both came out around the same time in 1994. Gary's book, *Obsession*, was more accurate and deeply researched while Eileen's book, *Breakdown*, was based on the unsupported premise that Bean-Bayog was guilty of sexual misconduct and that the big guns at Harvard Medical School were covering up for her. Eileen's book, however, was better written. She always did have a flair for the dramatic.

Jamie Lee Curtis never did do a movie about Margaret Bean-Bayog, nor did anyone else. Much later, I heard that Bean-Bayog died of leukemia in 2006, having never regained her medical license.

Chapter 16

A YEAR AFTER I returned from my second maternity leave, Spotlight, the *Globe*'s investigative team, decided to dig further into the issue of patient sexual abuse. Given my track record in covering this topic, Ben Bradlee, who had been promoted to Assistant Managing Editor in charge of special investigations, thought I'd be a natural fit to join the team. But Jerry O'Neill, the head of the Spotlight team at the time, was discomfited by my assertiveness. He told Bradlee that I wasn't enough of a "team player" and chose a younger, more compliant female reporter for the assignment. (In those days, Spotlight usually picked one woman for its four-person team to show how enlightened it was). The rebuff really stung. I did have a reputation for being outspoken, but I had worked on several articles with other reporters and had never had any problems. Toni Locy, the *Globe*'s court reporter, and I had enjoyed working together on an in-depth series about how then Governor William Weld's cuts in mental health were hurting Boston's homeless. I had also worked with David Armstrong, then an up-and coming-reporter, on a data-driven series about the enormous discrepancies in how different District Attorneys in Massachusetts enforced restraining orders on domestic violence cases and how those discrepancies often led to violence against women. This series was timed to run when O.J. Simpson went on trial for the murders of his ex-wife Nicole Simpson and her friend Ron Goldman. (Armstrong is now a highly respected investigative journalist at *ProPublica*.) I couldn't help thinking that a male reporter with a similar hard-charging approach would not have been treated like this. I remembered a study I had reported on several years prior about how assertive women couldn't win in the workplace. Looking back, my lede and first graph seemed rather prescient:

> Social psychologists now have hard evidence for what many working women already know: If you want to wield influence in a man's world, you have to play dumb. A new study has found that men are much more likely to have their minds changed by women who speak in a tentative, self-deprecating manner than by women who sound like they know what they're talking about.

My own editor, Nils Bruzelius, who had always been supportive of me, was away on a science journalism fellowship at the time. When I tried to discuss what happened with the Spotlight gig with another male editor whom I respected, all he said was, "Sorry, Alison, I don't do gender."

I decided I needed a change of scenery. Teresa Hanafin had been named Metro Editor and she had a reputation for mentoring other women. So I approached her about trying my hand as an editor on the city desk. She was enthusiastic and in 1996, I joined her team, editing dailies for the Metro section and whatever else was thrown my way. After a short stint on the desk, I was promoted to New England Editor, which meant that I was responsible for putting together our weekly New England section and editing daily stories from staff writers and freelancers covering western Massachusetts, Maine, and the four New England states that bordered Massachusetts. I was getting valuable management and editing experience, and I really enjoyed working with the talented freelancers who covered the New England region, several of whom ended up being hired full-time by the *Globe*.

One morning, I was asked to fill in for another editor at the editorial meeting that Matt Storin convened every morning to find out what stories the various departments (news, living, arts, sports, and business) were working on for the next day's paper. It also gave Storin the opportunity to critique articles that had appeared in the paper that day. We all sat around a conference table in one glassed-in corner of the newsroom with Storin at the head of the table flanked by his deputies.

That morning, he was incensed about something that Dan Duquette, then general manager of the Red Sox, had said in a sports roundup.

"This is fucked up," he roared. "We can't let him get away with this." Storin proceeded to repeatedly stab a copy of that day's *Boston Globe* with his pen.

As we watched our editor melt down, no one said a thing. I couldn't believe what I was seeing. The other editors, including grown men twice Storin's size, looked abashed, as if they were children being dressed down by an angry adult.

Finally, Larry Edelman, the Business Editor, said in a mild tone as if he were talking to a child, "Sounds like you're angry at Duquette."

But that only served to enrage Storin more. He continued to spew vitriol and finally stood up and stalked out of the room without finishing the meeting. Afterward, still shaken, I went up to another editor and asked whether this kind of thing happened on a regular basis. He acknowledged that it did.

"I feel like ducking under the desk when he loses it," said the editor, who was a good deal bigger and younger than Storin. "It makes me very uncomfortable."

"So why doesn't someone tell Storin that?" I asked. "Aren't you co-enabling this behavior by not saying anything?"

The editor glared at me. "I'm not co-enabling anything."

Over the next few days, I talked about Storin's behavior with a few of my co-workers and everyone agreed that his tantrums were counterproductive. Instead of encouraging the newsroom to take risks, which is what he said he wanted us to do, many editors and reporters were playing it safe. Anything to avoid being the target of his wrath. But no one seemed willing to say anything to him, as least as far as I knew. So I decided to do it. Why, you might ask, would I, a lowly editor on the city desk, willingly go into the lion's den and risk my career when more seasoned, high-ranking editors didn't seem willing to? I don't fully remember my thinking at the time, but I have always been far too willing to speak truth to power without thinking through the consequences. A mixture of hubris and stupidity, I suppose.

I made an appointment to see Storin. At the designated hour, I walked into his spacious corner office, which had wrap-around windows, a couch, and a small round conference table. Storin was sitting behind a huge mahogany desk and he gestured for me to sit in one of the chairs in front of his desk.

"Thanks for seeing me," I said. "I know you care deeply about the paper and want us to take risks and do our best work. But every time you lose your temper, it scares people and makes them more timid. And I know you don't want that." I was so nervous that I picked up a glass paperweight on his desk and ran my fingers around its smooth rounded edges.

"Are you going to throw that thing at me?" Storin asked.

I look at the paperweight in my hand in astonishment; I had never thrown anything at anyone in my life. At a previous newspaper gig, Storin had thrown a typewriter at someone else in a fit of rage. Was he projecting here? I hastily put the paperweight down.

"Oh no, sorry about that," I said. I tried to regain my composure, while Storin gazed at me with a small tight smile on his face. "As you know, I've worked for Nils Bruzelius for many years, and I think he's a very effective manager. He is not afraid to criticize us and he speaks his mind, but he also praises us when we do well, so we know he's on our side and . . . he never loses his temper."

Storin nodded curtly. "Yes, Nils is a good manager." He paused as if waiting for me to say something more, but I had finished my prepared speech. "I appreciate your coming in to talk to me. I'll think about what you said."

I walked out of his office in a daze, sensing that while Storin had been remarkably civil to me, perhaps because he was shocked by my temerity, I had just sabotaged my future at the *Globe*. It became obvious that Storin didn't like me. At one point, then Boston Mayor Thomas Menino was visiting the newsroom and I happened to be standing in a gaggle of editors standing around to meet him. Storin introduced me reluctantly and then turned to the woman standing right next to me and said, "And here's Renee Loth; we like *her*."

A few months later, I was sitting at my computer at the L-shaped city desk editing a story for deadline when out of the corner of my eye, I saw Matt Storin storming over. Close on his heels was Louisa Williams, an associate editor who functioned as his right-hand assistant.

"Who is this Michael Cohen?" Storin demanded. "Where the hell does he get off?"

Cohen was a talented freelancer who covered western Massachusetts for us. He had recently written several hard-hitting pieces about how General Electric was lobbying federal officials to forestall the government from designating its old plant on the Housatonic River as a Superfund site. Over the years, the GE factory had discharged a number of toxic metals and chemicals into the river, and soil for miles downstream of the plant was riddled with hazardous materials. Cohen had talked to a number of residents who lived along the river and complained that their children were getting sick as a result of the pollution. They wanted the riverbanks cleaned up. Once a particular site was designated a Superfund site by the federal Environmental Protection Agency, the responsible party, in this case, GE, was on the hook to spend millions of dollars to clean up the site.

I explained who Michael Cohen was and was just about to ask Storin what the problem was when Louisa Williams caught up with him. She laid a hand on his arm and said pleadingly, "Matt, you have a phone call in your office. I'll take care of this. Please."

Storin glared at me but without saying anything more, he turned on his heel and stalked off. Williams gave me a stern look and then she too walked away without saying a word. I later learned that Jack Welch, then the CEO of GE, had personally complained to Storin about our coverage of the proposed Superfund site. Louisa had talked to the Metro Editor and I was told not to commission any more articles about the GE Superfund controversy from Michael Cohen.

"Storin doesn't think he's covering the issue fairly," was how Teresa Hanafin explained it to me.

That particular episode left a bitter taste in my mouth. Tensions, in the meantime, had erupted in the newsroom between two different factions: those loyal to Mother Teresa, as our Metro Editor was called, and those who sided with Greg Moore, the paper's African-American managing editor. While Greg outranked Teresa, she had a strong base of support in Helen Donovan and Matt Storin, both of whom outranked Greg. So while Greg was not happy with the quality of the paper's local coverage, he couldn't just order Teresa to change things up. Teresa and Greg didn't much like or trust each other. Greg blamed her for being too parochial in her choice of Metro stories and not taking into account the city's growing racial and ethnic diversity. Greg even brought in an ally of his, Derrick Jackson, an editorial page writer, to work on the city desk for a few weeks and give Greg his assessment of what was wrong. It got to the point where Teresa was calling her staff in and asking what Derrick Jackson had talked to us about. I felt as though I was a pawn in the middle of a game of "I spy" that she and Greg Moore seemed to be playing. While I agreed with Greg that we weren't doing enough to cover the city's diverse population, Teresa had always been very supportive of me and I felt torn between my loyalty to her and my sense that our news coverage could use some help.

One afternoon, as I walked to the bathroom, I noticed that Robby, the former Metro Editor, was huddled with Executive Editor Helen Donovan in her glass-walled office. They were poring over something spread across Donovan's desk and their faces bore grim expressions. Jeez, I thought, something serious is going down but I had no idea what it was. As I and the entire newsroom were soon to find out, two of our star columnists were about to be exposed.

Chapter 17

EVER SINCE I joined the *Globe* in 1987, I had heard rumors that Mike Barnicle, the paper's star columnist, made stuff up. Fabricating sources, facts, and quotes and plagiarizing other people's work are cardinal sins in journalism and usually grounds for suspension or firing. According to the scuttlebutt in the newsroom, Barnicle was guilty of both. My sources at the paper told me that his editors knew about his transgressions but looked the other way because they thought the paper needed his voice. Barnicle had grown up in a working-class Irish family from Fitchburg, MA, and even though he now lived in the posh suburb of Lincoln and drove a BMW, he wrote as if he were still a working-class stiff. When Barnicle first started writing for the *Globe* in the early 1970s, the paper was being lambasted by the city's Irish population for supporting the desegregation of local schools. They denounced the *Globe* as a liberal rag that was pretty much a mouthpiece for its WASP owners. Barnicle provided the *Globe* with a welcome counterpoint to its supposed liberal bias, with his columns extolling working-class cops and firefighters and attacking what he derided as the wine and brie set who lived in Boston's tonier neighborhoods on Beacon Hill and Back Bay. A few years before I landed at the *Globe*, when I was living on the wrong side of Beacon Hill (back then that part of the Hill was still quite affordable), I wrote an angry letter to the paper denouncing one of Barnicle's attacks on the Beacon Hill "nobs who love brie." Personally, I hated brie and I was sick of Barnicle's stereotyping of anyone who wasn't working class and white. In that letter I wrote that I was cancelling my subscription to the *Globe* and I did. Instead, I subscribed to the *New York Times*.

After I joined the *Globe* (and re-subscribed to the paper), I don't recall Barnicle ever saying a word to me, although I saw him often enough, mostly standing around the circular desk where the telephone operators sat, jawing with the older women who answered the phones in the days before cell phones made landlines obsolete. Most of them were working-class Irish themselves, and they loved Barnicle and regularly parlayed juicy story tips to him, stroking his considerable ego in the process.

While I had little interaction with Barnicle, I was friendly with another Metro columnist, Patricia Smith, a talented African American writer and poetess. Matt Storin had known Smith when they both worked in Chicago and even before he returned to the *Globe*, had suggested the paper hire her. Smith was originally assigned to the Living section, where she wrote music reviews and vibrantly written features about musicians, novelists, and other interesting personalities in the arts. Storin was so impressed with her writing that he promoted her to Metro columnist in 1994. I liked Patricia Smith; she was smart and engaging and I, like many others in the newsroom, was blown away by her poetry.

But then in the late spring of 1998, Smith was caught fabricating sources in a number of her columns. As we later learned (not from our own management but from the extensive local coverage of the scandal), Smith had been caught doing the same thing two years prior, but rather than fire her, Storin had read her the riot act and allowed her to continue writing her column. When the whole thing blew up two years later, Storin told a local magazine writer that he felt that he had to give Patricia Smith a second chance because of all second chances Barnicle had been given over the years for essentially doing the same thing. As *Boston Magazine* writer Sean Flynn wrote, "Storin realized that if he fired Smith, he risked a racial schism not only in his newsroom, but among the *Globe*'s million or so readers."

Storin not only forgave Smith's egregious lapses; despite the evidence of Smith's fabrication, he submitted several of her columns for the Pulitzer Prize the next year. She didn't win the brass ring but emerged as one of three finalists for commentary in March 1998. Perhaps that honor emboldened her because in May of the same year, Smith wrote a questionable column about "Claire," a woman who was dying of cancer and desperate for a miracle cure. Claire, like the rest of the literate public, had heard that Dr. Judah Folkman, in his lab at Children's Hospital, had discovered two drugs that apparently killed cancer cells in mice and made their tumors disappear. Researchers around the country were excited about the new finding and Nobel Laureate James Watson was even quoted in the *New York Times* saying that "Judah is going to cure cancer in two years." In her May 11 column, Patricia Smith quoted Claire as saying, "Hell, if I could get my hands on [the drug], I'd swallow the whole . . . mouse."

To Robby and others in the newsroom, the quote sounded too perfect, the woman's identity too vague. He relayed his concerns to Helen Donovan and she gave him permission to check out Smith's columns again. It didn't take Robby long to discover that not only could he find no evidence of a Claire dying of cancer but in examining other Smith columns, he found a number of other sources he couldn't trace.

On June 17, Patricia Smith admitted to Greg Moore, who was her editor, that four of the individuals she wrote about in her recent columns, including Claire, the cancer patient, were fabricated.

The next morning, we in the newsroom were summoned to a staff meeting in the William O. Taylor room, a small auditorium off of the paper's main lobby, where Storin announced Smith's resignation. I was stunned. I had had no idea she made up facts. While I understood that Smith needed to be let go, I was furious at the *Globe*'s double standard in turning a blind eye to Barnicle's long history of journalistic transgressions.

Some prominent readers were also weighing in on the *Globe*'s double standard in firing Patricia Smith but allowing Mike Barnicle to slide by. In a statement faxed to media outlets, Alan Dershowitz, a Harvard law professor whom Barnicle had allegedly misquoted (the *Globe* had earlier forked over a generous sum in a libel suit Dershowitz brought against Barnicle) asserted that a black woman was losing her job for transgressions a white man had gotten away with for years. Yet despite such sentiments, Barnicle seemed untouchable.

It was around this time that I decided I no longer wanted to be part of a newsroom that sanctioned such hypocrisy. I also hated the infighting and the late hours I had to put in every night editing late-breaking stories, especially on Friday evenings when we were putting the New England section to bed and preparing other stories for the Sunday paper. I wasn't leaving work until eight or nine at night, well after my two sons, then in kindergarten and elementary school, had gone to bed, and I missed reading them a good night story and tucking them in. Sometime in late June or early July, I asked Executive Editor Helen Donovan if I could transfer to the Living section, which had more family-friendly hours. I had a good relationship with Helen; she respected me as a journalist and I respected her as a gifted manager of people, someone who worked hard at soothing ruffled feathers and bringing out the best in *Globe* employees.

I was still working in the newsroom in early August, when Mike Barnicle finally self-destructed. While out of town on a trip, he filed a quick column full of funny and not so funny one-liners. Within days, the *Boston Herald* broke the news that eight of Barnicle's jokes were virtually identical to one-liners in a book by comedian George Carlin (Barnicle hadn't credited Carlin or anyone else in his column). At that point Storin felt he had to act, so he suspended Barnicle for a month. Then it turned out that Barnicle had lied when he told *Globe* editors he had never read Carlin's book. *Channel 5* ran a clip of him recommending it on *Chronicle,* a show on which Barnicle was a regular contributor. Storin finally demanded Barnicle's resignation.

But even that wasn't the end of it. Barnicle fought back, mounting a media offensive to convince Storin to change his mind. He also had an important ally at the paper—the paper's publisher, Ben Taylor. Barnicle personally pled his case with Taylor and the upshot was that Storin announced that Barnicle would remain on staff following a two-month suspension. And that's where matters might have stood if the former top editor for *Reader's Digest* had not come forward. He wrote a letter to Matt Storin in August 1998 informing him that his staff at the *Readers Digest,* which fact checks every article before they reprint, could not verify Barnicle's October 8, 1995 column. I happened to know firsthand how extensively the *Readers Digest* fact checks articles because they wanted to reprint an in-depth piece I had written for the *Globe* magazine in 1996 about the health effects of anger and the different ways an angry outburst by a man or woman is viewed. The *Readers Digest* editor had asked me for every single one of my sources for the article, their names and contact numbers, as well as the studies I had cited, so they could fact check the piece before running it. Everything must have checked out because my anger piece was reprinted in *Readers Digest* and I received a $150 check for the reprint.

Apparently, the *Readers Digest* editor who had been fact checking Barnicle's 1995 column had also called him to request contact information for his sources, but Barnicle refused to help. According to the letter Storin received on August 18, the *Readers Digest* editors couldn't find any of the sources Barnicle quoted in his column. They came to the conclusion that the sources had been fabricated and decided not to reprint his column.

Upon receipt of this damning letter, Storin asked Robby to look into the matter. He couldn't verify the sources or story Barnicle relayed in his 1995 column either. That was the last straw. Storin again demanded Barnicle's resignation, and he finally submitted it in a phone call to *Globe* chairman William O. Taylor, who had been publisher of the paper before his cousin assumed that role.

In August, I was on vacation when Storin once again gathered the newsroom and announced Barnicle's departure. But according to friends of mine who were there, the reporters and editors in attendance all broke out in applause. The *Globe* was finally doing the right thing in banishing its ethical ghosts.

Chapter 18

BY THE END of August 1998, Helen Donovan had worked her magic and I was transferred to the Living section, where my assignment was to write long features and profiles. I was incredibly relieved to be out of newsroom maelstrom. I got along fine with Nick King, the Living editor, who was a respected journalist and pretty much let me come up with my own story ideas, although now and then he assigned me to do a piece. One of the first stories I did was about a sixty-year-old convicted sex offender who had done his prison time and was trying to live out the rest of his life in peace. The man had not reoffended, but he was being regularly harassed by angry intruders who would park in his driveway, honk at him, flash their high beams, and throw things on his lawn. The headline of the story was "No Peace for a Pariah," and my article raised the question: "When, if ever, can a criminal finish repaying his debt and gain redemption?"

Nick loved that piece and played it prominently on the front of the Living section. But he was not so happy with another story I wrote (at his urging) about the Landmark Forum. The Forum is an updated version of est, the self-help movement in the 1970s that drew criticism for fostering an authoritarian atmosphere, with reports of est leaders humiliating participants and refusing to let them go to the bathroom.

My assignment was to attend one of the Forum's weekend immersion events, held in Boston, and write about the experience. Nick, I think, was hoping that I would tear into the organization and expose it as a sham that took vulnerable people's money and did nothing for them. But the Forum's message of taking personal responsibility for your actions and reconciling with friends and family members you've had differences with resonated with me and many others who attended the weekend symposium. As one participant joked, it was a "kinder, gentler est" where anyone could leave at any time and people were encouraged to confront the ways in which their own behavior had contributed to problems in their relationships. Over the weekend, I (along with other Forum participants) ended up writing letters to people in my life, asking their forgiveness for times I had been less than patient or understanding of them. The lengthy feature I wrote (which gave the Forum experience mixed reviews) was not quite the exposé Nick wanted.

Even so, Nick and I got along fine and I enjoyed working in Living until he became magazine editor and we got a new editor who had been Nick's assistant editor. Fiona, who was in her thirties, had worked her way up at the *Globe* from being a Night Desk Copy Editor to Food Editor, and she was less secure about her authority than Nick had been. She had never been a reporter and she didn't like reporters pushing back against her wishes.

In the fall of 1999, I opened a package addressed to me to find copies of tax returns for Dr. Martin Keller, the chair of psychiatry at Brown University. I had written several investigative articles in the mid-nineties about how Keller's psychiatry department at Brown had received thousands of dollars in funding from the Massachusetts Department of Mental Health (DMH) for research it wasn't conducting. A source who worked in Keller's department had given me internal documents showing that Keller's staff had even falsified invoices to the DMH in order to continue to receive funding for research that was supposed to be conducted on schizophrenic patients at a clinic in Fall River, MA. But no research occurred there during the years cited in the invoices, according to the very researchers whose names were on the invoices as doing the work. The head of DMH, who had initially told me her agency did not have a contract with anyone at Brown, was nonplussed to find out that her department was indeed funding a wealthy Ivy League research institution at a time when it was cutting vital services for the mentally ill in Massachusetts. As I discovered while literally digging through files at the state mental health agency, the contract with Keller's department at Brown was hidden inside another contract DMH had with the Fall River clinic in question.

After my page-one article was published in January 1996, the commissioner put an immediate stop to the funding. Later that year, the Massachusetts Attorney General even sued Brown in an effort to recoup the $218,000 in funding. I soon followed that piece up with another story about how Keller had double billed both Brown and the drug companies for whom he was consulting for his travel expenses and gotten reimbursed twice.

Now, some three years later, I was excited to get copies of Keller's tax returns for several years, especially since tax returns are not publicly available documents. I soon realized their significance: they showed that Keller had received hundreds of thousands of dollars in personal income from various pharmaceutical companies, money he had not disclosed (as required) to either Brown or the National Institute of Mental Health, with whom he had a number of major research grants. At the time, little had been written about the financial conflicts of interest that many medical researchers failed to disclose, conflicts that made these researchers beholden to the very companies whose drugs they were evaluating. Studies showed that such large sums of money often compromised the independence and credibility of researchers' findings.

When I went to Fiona to tell her about the Keller story and ask her for a few days to report on it, she refused to let me do the story.

"You're supposed to be writing features," Fiona said. "You need to turn this over to someone in the health and science section."

I couldn't believe my ears. I was the *Globe* reporter most knowledgeable about Keller and his financial conflicts of interest and the tip had come directly to me. I knew that Dick Lehr, a male reporter in the Living section, was regularly allowed to work on investigative stories even though he ostensibly reported to Fiona. Lehr was a gifted writer and although he was assigned to Living, he often worked with Jerry O'Neill, the Spotlight editor, on articles about Whitey Bulger and the Boston mob. Lehr also wrote the occasional Living feature. Indeed, it was while Lehr was in Living that he and O'Neill wrote their groundbreaking book about Bulger and the Irish mafia, *Black Mass,* which was later made into a movie with Johnny Depp.

When Fiona told me I couldn't do the Keller story, I said I wanted to discuss this with Mary Jane Wilkinson, the Living/Arts Editor and Fiona's superior. Fiona didn't like that one bit, but she agreed and the two of us met with Mary Jane, who was obviously caught in a tough place. I could tell she agreed with me that it was only fair that I follow up on the Keller story. But she also felt she had to support Fiona. So after we both said our piece, Mary Jane reached a Solomonic decision. She said I could do this one article about Keller but would have to turn any follow-up stories over to another reporter.

My story about Keller and the hundreds of thousands of dollars he was secretly receiving from Big Pharma ran on page one of the *Globe* October 4, 1999. It created such a groundswell of outrage that officials at NIH began looking into the story and re-examining their conflict-of-interest policies. As agreed upon, I turned the reporting for the follow-up story over to Dolores Kong, a health reporter. I told her who to call and how to report the story but she did the legwork and wrote it. But then I made a big mistake. Dolores, being the generous, conscientious reporter that she was, said she really wanted to give me a double byline on the piece. After all, it was my story and she felt I should get some credit for it. Even though I knew I shouldn't have said yes, I agreed.

When Fiona saw my name on the double byline, she flipped out. She ran to the top editors and demanded that I be removed from Living. She obviously considered the double byline a direct attack on her authority and wanted me gone. Since I was still working on a number of in-depth features, I was allowed to stay in Living for a few more months. But by early 2000, I found out I was being transferred back to the main newsroom as a general assignment reporter, which meant I would be on call to cover any assignment the city desk wanted to give me. After so many years of mostly deciding my own assignments, I essentially was being banished to purgatory. I would no longer be able to control my schedule and would once again have to work late hours that took me away from my family.

If Matt Storin had been in my corner, he might have backed me up but because of my earlier confrontation with him, Storin was no fan of mine. I tried to tell my side of the story to Helen Donovan, but she was no longer listening. Greg Moore, who was Fiona's mentor and had brought her onto the paper as a minority hire (she was of Filipino background), must have convinced Helen that they had to back Fiona up. At one point in our conversation, Helen said that I didn't know how to take no for an answer.

"I know that makes you a good journalist, but editors need to know their authority is being respected," she said.

What she meant but didn't say was that I was being punished for not sufficiently deferring to Fiona's authority. I had published a major page-one story about conflicts of interest in medicine that was prompting the National Institutes of Health to re-examine their conflicts of interest policy with researchers. I had broken the Father Porter story and a host of other important stories and had even come close to winning a Pulitzer for my series on psychiatrists who had sex with their patients. But in management's view, I was now a troublemaker and needed to be punished. I had gotten on the bad side of an editor whom top management liked and wanted to hold onto. She was the rising star, not me. The *Globe*, I realized, no longer had my back.

Being demoted to a general assignment reporter was humiliating; it felt as if all my colleagues were witnessing my demotion and shame. I knew I had to get out of there or I would go insane. I was already starting to lose it. I remember trying to hide from the city desk by stacking books and papers as high as possible on my newly assigned desk so the city desk editors couldn't see me. This was not exactly the behavior of a rational person.

Within weeks, I had found another job: as Executive Editor for *CIO* magazine, a trade publication for the IT industry based in Framingham. If I had known that Matt Storin would be shown the door less than a year later and Marty Baron brought in as the *Globe*'s new editor, I might have tried to hang on. But at the time I was furious at the way I was being treated and embarrassed that I hadn't handled the situation better. I should have understood perhaps that Fiona, in her first big job at the paper, needed more deference than I had shown my previous editors. But political savvy has never been my strong suit. The *Globe* had been my calling and my family for thirteen years, and I had cared enough about the paper to walk into the top editor's office and tell him his anger issues were getting in the way of an effective newsroom. But none of that mattered now. My friends at the paper threw me a farewell lunch, and my last day on the job was June 30, 2000. In the privacy of my car, I cried the whole way home.

Chapter 19

SEVERAL MONTHS BEFORE I left the *Globe*, I had stumbled across what I thought would make a great idea for a book. In the course of reporting a feature on the freewheeling mix of work and play that typified life at dot-com companies in the Boston area, I had chanced across something very unusual: the female CEO of an internet startup. Ilene Lang had developed AltaVista, the very first commercial internet search engine, while working at Digital Equipment Corp., a computer company in Massachusetts. AltaVista could have become Google had Lang had the backing of her bosses at Digital. But like many older white men (including the publisher of the *Boston Globe* who had the opportunity to invest in monster.com but didn't take it), Lang's bosses didn't have the foresight to envision what the internet would become. Nor did they take Lang, the only woman in their executive suite, seriously. They declined to put up the money needed to develop AltaVista into a full-fledged search engine. Their tunnel vision cost them big. Alta Vista was quickly eclipsed by other search engines and DEC itself was sold to another computer company and disappeared from sight. Eileen Lang went on to become CEO of another promising internet startup, a company called Individual that specialized in online business news. I thought her story, as one of the few female executives in the high-flying dot-com world, would make a great book.

Lang allowed me to shadow her at her office and when she gave talks around town. One morning, I sat in on a pivotal meeting about her startup's future. It was 10 am on a sunny day in December 1999, and she had asked all of her employees to attend. Lang was running on four cups of coffee and three hours of sleep. But despite the deep circles beneath her eyes, she appeared relaxed and confident, her usual upbeat self.

"Never a dull moment around here, huh?" Lang quipped to the staff members who crowded around her on chairs and windowsills. She then announced that NewsEdge, Individual's parent company, was being acquired by another Cambridge-based firm. But that company had no interest in supporting Individual.

"I've talked Rowe into letting me sell Individual," Lang said. "While it looks very scary at the moment, this is actually good news. We can now do a deal that the investors want to do and do it quickly."

Lang told her assembled troops that she had talked to four companies and each one has expressed strong interest in acquiring Individual. It was just a matter of putting a deal together. When Lang ended the meeting ninety minutes later, Individual's employees dispersed to their lavender-gray cubicles, content in the belief that their boss, as usual, had everything under control.

In the early spring of 2000, I wrote up a book proposal about a female CEO of an internet startup who had overcome tremendous odds to get where she was. But before my literary agent could sell the book, the dot-com bubble burst and suddenly no one was interested in a book that had anything to do with the dot-com world. I was devastated. In those years, the *Boston Globe* automatically gave anyone with a book contract a sabbatical to write it, and I had hoped such a sabbatical would save me from being demoted. But that wasn't to be.

After I left the paper, I managed to sell Ilene Lang's story to my old editor at Living, who was now the editor of the *Globe* magazine. It ran as the cover story of the magazine on July 22, 2001, but the central premise had been changed at the insistence of my editor. Lang was no longer depicted as the successful CEO of a high-flying startup, but as a wife, mother, and executive whose single-minded drive had destroyed her marriage. The headline was "Wife, mother, high-tech exec, Ilene Lang had it all. Or did she? The choices she made." My article still portrayed Lang as a success story—after all, she had managed to sell Individual.com at an inflated price with big stock wins for herself and her employees just three months before the dot-com bubble burst. But I had to revise the story to suit Nick's requirements and get it published. While every word was accurate—Ilene had opened up to me to an astonishing degree, thinking she would be the subject of a book—the focus was on her lifestyle and the choices she had made to achieve success. I even talked to her ex-husband, who acknowledged feeling abandoned because of Lang's devotion to her career.

Lang, understandably, was upset with the new angle of the piece. In an email to me and my editor, she said she doubted the *Globe* would have run a similar cover story about a hard-driving male CEO whose marriage had faltered. The headline of the story and the emphasis on her divorce, she said, was sexist. And she was right; the *Globe* would never have published a similarly in-depth piece about a male CEO whose marriage had fallen apart because of his single-minded devotion to work. Not then, and probably not even now. It is still a man's world and successful men are rarely questioned about their choices regarding work and family. I felt terrible and apologized to Eileen via email and several messages left on her phone. But I never heard from her again. My sense of guilt was only partially assuaged a few years later upon reading in the *New York Times* wedding announcements that Ilene had married her high school sweetheart. He had reconnected with her after reading my 2001 *Globe* magazine article about her.

For the first few years I worked at *CIO,* a trade publication for chief information officers, the magazine was flying high. Craigslist, Google, and Facebook had not yet destroyed the business model for glossy print magazines (or newspapers), and I had the chance to travel first-class to conferences and do interviews with famous tech personalities. I enjoyed the work, writing and editing in-depth features about cyberespionage and the FBI's ineptitude with cyber technology, among many other topics. I had received a hefty salary increase to join the magazine and I liked working with the talented group of younger reporters the magazine also hired. For the first time, *CIO* became a finalist for the coveted National Magazine of the Year award from the American Society of Magazine Editors for issues I had edited and written for. We also won two Grand Neal awards, the most prestigious editorial honors in the field of business-to-business journalism, for stories I had conceived and edited.

In 2002, my bosses gave me permission to teach a science journalism class to graduate students at Boston University. One afternoon a week, I left work early and drove into Boston to teach the three-hour class. I discovered that I enjoyed teaching and hoped to continue doing it.

I also appreciated the fact that I could leave work by 5 pm almost every evening and spend more time with my two boys, then eleven and eight. I was still coaching my younger son's Newton Youth soccer team (I had also coached my older son's team until he was eleven and graduated to a more experienced coach). And I was able to attend more of their games and school events than I had ever been able to before. The summer of 2001, the four of us went on a two-week trip to Colorado and the Grand Canyon, where we rode horses and hiked down steep trails that catapulted my heart into my throat for fear one of the boys would slip and fall into the abyss. But even nine-year-old Jakie managed to keep his footing (even though we had accidentally left his new hiking boots at his aunt's house in Colorado and he was wearing worn-out sneakers.) On a side trip to Mesa Verde, I experienced a sudden attack of vertigo, which made me freeze on a ladder climbing from one cliffside cave to another. The guide eventually got me moving, but I never did hear the end of it from my boys. It was probably the first time they had seen their usually indomitable mother paralyzed by fear.

In June 2004, I was sitting on my couch at home reading the *Sunday New York Times* when a page-one story caught my eye. The New York state attorney general's office had just filed suit against GlaxoSmithKline, accusing the second largest pharmaceutical company in the world of consumer fraud for not revealing all of its data about the antidepressant Paxil. Paxil was one of a new class of antidepressants that worked a different way than older antidepressants. Known as selective serotonin reuptake inhibitors (SSRIs), because they supposedly interfered with chemicals in the brain that induced depression, these drugs included Prozac, Zoloft, Paxil, and, later, Celexa and Lexapro. When the SSRIs first hit the market, pharm companies marketed them as safer and more effective than older anti-depression drugs, and many doctors hailed them as magic bullets.

As the story I was reading revealed, Glaxo had refused to allow the publication of a clinical trial about Paxil that found it no more effective than a placebo in treating depression in adolescents. At the same time, the company had vigorously promoted the publication of another clinical trial, which allegedly found that Paxil was safe and effective in treating depression in kids. And the lead investigator of that published trial was none other than Dr. Martin Keller, the chair of psychiatry at Brown University. I almost fell off the couch. This was the same researcher I had exposed earlier for failing to disclose the hundreds of thousands of dollars in personal income he received from pharmaceutical companies. Seeing Keller's name in the paper sent a jolt of adrenaline coursing through me.

I had first heard of Keller and his misdeeds from a woman who worked in his psychiatry department, an administrator by the name of Donna Howard. In December 1995, Donna had left an anonymous message with the *Globe* city desk, something about the misappropriation of funds from a state mental health agency. It was forwarded to me as the paper's mental health reporter. It was late in the afternoon when I got the message, and I was spent, having just filed a story for the next day's paper. But something prompted me to return the call. Donna explained that she was the assistant administrator for Brown University's Department of Psychiatry and had in her possession documents proving that the department was getting paid hundreds of thousands of dollars from the Massachusetts Department of Mental Health for research that wasn't being done. She said she also suspected that Martin Keller and other researchers in his department were misrepresenting data for two drug trials. I remember typing quick notes, my phone cradled to one ear, thinking this couldn't be for real.

Donna and I agreed to meet the next day at a Burger King on Route 24. She suggested the restaurant because it was halfway between Providence (where Brown is situated) and Boston. Donna was already there when I arrived, seated in a small corner booth with a big cardboard box full of documents by her side. She said she had come forward because she had a daughter with mental illness and was outraged that a financially strapped state agency was apparently giving a wealthy institution like Brown money under false pretenses. She said she also was concerned about the possible skewing of research data in two large, randomized drug trials being conducted at Brown. One of the trials involved studying the effectiveness of the antidepressant Paxil in adolescents.

Based on what Donna and others told me, I wrote a series of articles in the *Boston Globe* about research and billing transgressions by Brown University's chief of psychiatry. Three years later, my article about Martin Keller's tax returns and his failure to disclose his extensive conflicts of interest hit the stands. As with my first page-one piece about Keller, there were calls for investigations. In the end, neither Brown nor the NIH took any disciplinary action against him.

As I sat on my couch that day in 2004 reading the *New York Times* article with growing excitement, I remembered what Donna Howard had told me almost nine years prior. Back then, I hadn't been able to pin down her allegations about Keller's Paxil study. But now it appeared as though the New York State Attorney General's office had done it for me. I had to find out more; could this be the book I was meant to write?

With a few phone calls, I discovered that the Glaxo lawsuit was the brainchild of Rose Firestein, a feisty newcomer to Attorney General Eliot Spitzer's office. Rose agreed to talk to me, so I took a vacation day and flew down to New York City. The New York State Attorney's office was in the financial district of Lower Manhattan, very close to where the World Trade Center buildings had once stood. On my way to Rose's office, I paused by the yawning open pit at Ground Zero and was accosted by the sudden memory of standing on top of the north tower with my family nine months before its collapse, a chill wind blowing through my hair.

As soon as I met Rose Firestein, I knew I had a great book in the making. She was the antithesis of the formidable-looking investigative lawyers you often see in the movies. Rose was short, legally blind, and walked with a cane. Yet she turned out to be one of the smartest, toughest do-gooders I've ever met. She also had a big heart. The very first time I spoke to Rose, she said she knew of my work. Her exact words were: "I just want you to know how much I appreciate your articles. When I read your pieces about Keller, they made me look at psychiatry in a whole different light. I had not realized before the depth of the connection between academic researchers and the pharmaceutical industry."

As an assistant attorney general, Rose had subpoena power and in preparing her lawsuit against GlaxoSmithKline, she had subpoenaed hundreds of confidential corporate documents about the company's off-label promotion of Paxil for use in children and adolescents. It is against the law for drug companies to market drugs for off-label use, i.e. to promote drugs for uses that had not been officially approved by the FDA. While the FDA had approved Paxil, along with other SSRI antidepressants for use in treating adult depression, it had not officially sanctioned their use in minors. Doctors, of course, can legally prescribe for off-label uses, but drug companies are not allowed to market drugs for them. Rose had hit upon a novel legal strategy in going after Glaxo for its off-label promotion of Paxil: she argued that the drug company was defrauding consumers by publishing only one study of Paxil and hiding other studies that found no benefit from the drug.

And that was only part of the story. Among the boxes I had dragged home when I left the *Globe* was one filled with internal Brown University documents that Donna Howard had turned over to me when we met that afternoon at Burger King. In that treasure trove, I found documents that appeared to show that the one clinical trial of Paxil in teenagers that Glaxo promoted as a positive finding—the study spearheaded by Martin Keller—did not actually find anything of the sort. By then, Glaxo had settled with the New York Attorney General in part by promising to put all of its raw data from the Paxil study 329, as the Brown trial was known, along with data from its other studies, online as part of a new online clinical registry. I was thus able to match the documents I had in my personal possession with the raw data that Keller and other researchers turned over to Glaxo.

What I discovered was mind-boggling. The internal memos I had kept in my basement all those years showed that Brown researchers had lied about the science to make Paxil look safer and more effective in children than it really was. For example, the documents showed that the findings about several of the adolescents in the study were miscoded to make it look as though their suicidal and aggressive tendencies had nothing to do with their being on Paxil. One teenager in the Brown trial had been discharged from the study for combative behavior, when she should have been included in the study group considered suicidal as a result of taking Paxil.

While I was researching my book, I discovered that the FDA had undertaken its own analysis of the raw data in study 329 and reached the same conclusion I had: that the trial was not a positive finding after all. The study had actually found that Paxil was not safe and effective in treating depression in minors; in fact, its data showed that Paxil caused a four-fold increase in suicidal thoughts and behaviors among adolescents in that study compared to those taking the placebo.

I made several trips to New York to interview not only Rose Firestein but her colleagues at the New York Attorney General's office. And in August 2005, I drove to Albany to interview the big boss, New York Attorney General Eliot Spitzer, who had already announced plans to run for governor of New York the following year.

Spitzer's office was in the Capitol building, an ornate castle-like structure with marble columns, intricately carved gargoyles, and high vaulted ceilings. I had been instructed to go first to the office of Spitzer's press handler, Marc Violette, whom I had been in touch with to set up the interview. While Marc's office on the second floor was tiny, Spitzer's office was huge and wood-paneled with book-lined shelves, gleaming cherry furniture, and antique lamps. An oriental rug adorned the hardwood floor.

I was shown to a small oval conference table and joined by Violette and Tom Conway, who was head of the AG's consumer protection bureau and Firestein's boss. Conway was a tall, lanky man who could be brusque with his subordinates but knew just when to break the ice with a joke or funny story. Marc, Tom, and I made some small talk because Spitzer himself was just finishing up a phone call. I couldn't help but admire the AG's energy, as he paced around his huge mahogany desk talking into the phone, wearing a crisp tailored white shirt, maroon tie, and charcoal pants.

"Sorry for making you wait," he said after he had finished his call and joined us at the table. Up close, Spitzer had piercing blue-green eyes and a shy smile. When I asked what he thought when he first heard about the case the lawyers in his consumer protection division were considering bringing against GlaxoSmithKline, he nodded intently.

"I remember thinking it was an amazing case and was so clearly the right thing to do," Spitzer said. "This isn't about money. As bad as all the Wall Street [financial conflict of interest] cases were, that's money. This is about somebody's health, where the downside consequences of mischaracterizing what the impact of a particular drug is are dramatically more important and so I expected a greater degree of care than what we saw."

As we talked, Spitzer pointed out that GlaxoSmithKline's lawyers very quickly agreed to come to the table after his office filed the case. "What motivated them was probably the reality that they knew we were right, and they had been caught in a very uncomfortable position."

Glaxo's lawyers, he added, were surprised that his office didn't want a pile of money; instead the Attorney General wanted the drug company to change its behavior and disclose all of its clinical data from here on in, so that it and other pharmaceutical companies could no longer easily misrepresent the science behind new drugs. Spitzer said he didn't understand why the FDA hadn't already required such disclosures of drug companies (and still doesn't to this day.)

"The medical journals [that publish the results of drug trials] would not be vulnerable to mischaracterization if they had access to the data," he said. "It still mystifies me why the FDA has not done that."

Spitzer went on to say that his team had done "an amazing job" in bringing the Paxil case and he was very proud of them. I remember thinking two things about Eliot Spitzer: he was very sure of himself, and he was going places.

In gathering material for my book, I also sought out Donna Howard again and interviewed her about her growing misgivings over the Paxil trial and why she decided to drop the dime on Marty Keller. In addition, I interviewed Dr. Martin Teicher, a psychiatrist at McLean

Hospital, who was among the first doctors in the nation to raise the alarm about what looked like a serious side effect of Prozac, the first SSRI antidepressant to hit the market. Teicher, a noted researcher and clinician who played in a band and composed his own music, had discovered that some of his patients, after taking Prozac, expressed suicidal thoughts they'd never had before. He and two colleagues at McLean Hospital wrote up a case report noting that about 3.5 percent of a hundred and seventy patients under their care had developed an intense and sometimes violent preoccupation with suicide. The report was published in the *American Journal of Psychiatry,* and Eli Lilly, the maker of Prozac, was furious. When Teicher agreed to testify a few years later in a lawsuit against Eli Lilly brought by the widow of a prominent attorney, who had killed himself after taking Prozac, the drug company tried to smear his reputation. Its attorneys brought up allegations that a seriously depressed patient of Teicher had made, accusing the psychiatrist of having sexual relations with her while he was treating her. Those allegations were never substantiated—like Paul Lozano, the medical student who had killed himself after being treated by Margaret Bean-Bayog, the female patient who accused Teicher of misconduct had been sexually abused as a child and was very troubled. But that didn't stop Eli Lilly from using the allegations to intimidate Teicher when he testified about the dangers of Prozac during the widow's court case.

I knew I had some amazing material for a book, and Ike, the agent who had tried to sell my book on Ilene Lang, agreed. He turned my book proposal (which consisted of a sample chapter, a chapter outline, and a book overview) over to one of his new agents, a young woman with relatively little experience who worked in New York City. She sent out the proposal to a list of publishers, but no one bit. I was terribly disappointed. What could I do, I asked her, to get the book sold? She suggested I revise the proposal to make the narrative more suspenseful and agreed to contact more publishers when I was done with the revision.

In the midst of all this, the parent company of *CIO* decided to fold a new magazine it had launched called *CMO* (aimed at chief marketing officers). In retrospect, its decision to launch a new startup on the eve of the internet juggernaut that would soon destroy the business model of print magazines and newspapers may have seemed foolhardy. But then again, very few people in the media saw it coming.

A month or so later, in September 2005, the company carried out a massive layoff. I had no idea what was going on until I bumped into one of my colleagues in the bathroom that morning. Mindy was dabbing at her eyes in front of the mirror; it was obvious she had been crying.

"I've just been laid off, can you believe it?" Mindy said. "They want me out of here in an hour. After all I've done for this company!"

My mouth dropped open. "What! That's not fair!"

Mindy nodded angrily. "They're laying off everyone who works for *CMO* and then some. It's horrible!"

My head spinning, I left the ladies room and walked in a daze back to my cubicle. As I passed my boss's office, Abbie was standing near the door and she gestured me inside. Oh my god, I thought, I'm going to be laid off too! Sick to my stomach, I shuffled into her office as if I was going to an execution.

"Am I going to be laid off too?" I blurted out, too upset to mince words.

Abbie shook her head wearily. "No, but others are. I know it's awful but it has to be done. Keep your head down."

As I learned later, a lot of older employees who were making good salaries were laid off that day: the head of marketing, the head of events planning, and one of our best fact checkers, a woman by the name of Carol, who was in her fifties. She had just completed a course in chemotherapy for breast cancer.

One of my favorite graphic designers was also let go. Neva had managed to emigrate to the U.S. from Bulgaria without her family and she was a spunky, talented young woman. After the Human Resources rep told her she was being laid off, he had the temerity to ask Neva how she felt. She replied, "You don't care how I feel. Just tell me what I need to know to get out of here." Neva, I knew would land her feet, but I would miss her plucky attitude.

Another of the writers who was laid off that day happened to share the four-desk cubicle I worked in. In the span of an hour, I watched

Chris, a talented writer and hard worker with a great sense of humor, go from shock and outrage to acceptance.

"You know, this will give me the opportunity to do some things I really want to try—like teaching," he finally said, as he gathered up his box of belongings and prepared to leave. Like the other laid-off employees, Chris had already been locked out of his computer; that was the first thing the company did even as Chris and others were being told they were laid off.

"In a weird kind of way, I feel liberated," he said, and then after allowing me to give him a quick hug, he picked up his box and walked out of my life.

As I sat at my desk, too numb to do any work, I thought about how inhumane my company was being. None of the laid-off employees were going to create havoc online; they were decent people and should have been given the chance to say good-bye to their colleagues and get their affairs in order without being shown the door within an hour by security personnel. I had to get out of there, I thought. I didn't want to work for a company that treated human beings like cattle. I redoubled my efforts to revise the book proposal and sent the new version off to my agent by the end of September, fingers crossed.

Chapter 20

MY LITERARY AGENT didn't have any luck with her next round of submissions to publishers. Right before the Christmas holidays in 2005, she called and told me that my proposal just wasn't book material and I should come up with another idea. I was devastated. I had poured my heart and soul and eighteen months into researching this book and she was telling me to forget about it. Move on. The holidays that year were a very bleak time for me. Even my son, David, who wanted nothing to do with his parents at the rebellious age of sixteen, noticed how subdued I was.

One evening he came over to give me a hug.

"Are you okay, Mom?" David said. "I'm worried about you."

I gave him a tired smile. "I'll be fine, David. Don't worry. Your mother is a tough cookie."

David grinned. "I know that, Mom. Just don't give up."

Sometime around the New Year, I confided my woes to a friend of mine, Laura Van Dam, who was science editor at Houghton Mifflin, a textbook publisher in Boston, and had just been elected president of the National Association of Science Writers. Laura and I had worked together at *Technology Review* magazine years before and we remained friendly. She threw a baby shower for my first child, and I returned the favor by throwing her a baby shower. Her son, also named David, was born three months after my David. After looking over my proposal, Laura reassured me that it would make a great book and suggested I get in touch with another New York agent she knew, Jim Levine.

Jim read my proposal, liked it, and suggested I write a second chapter, which I did. He then sent my revised proposal out to a number of agents in February 2006 and within three weeks, I had a book contract—with Algonquin Books, a trade press in New York City.

To say I was ecstatic puts it mildly. Finally, I had the chance to write a creative nonfiction narrative that told an important story, about how the pharmaceutical industry handsomely rewards some researchers to make their drugs look safer and more effective than they really are.

There was only one problem: my boss at *CIO* turned down my request for a six-month unpaid sabbatical to write the book. I knew it would take me longer to finish the book, but I figured I could get a lot done in six months of writing full time. However, we had a relatively small staff and Abbie felt that she couldn't spare me even for six months. What was I going to do? I knew that my editors at Algonquin wanted the book as soon as possible. I had received a modest advance of $40,000 (half when the contract was signed and the other half when the book was finished). But that wouldn't come close to defraying the loss of my salary.

I talked it over with my husband and we decided we could temporarily get by on his income as a social worker and what little savings we had. In the meantime, I would apply for an Alicia Patterson Fellowship, a prestigious journalism fellowship that at that time gave selected fellows an annual stipend of $35,000, and we would hope for the best. In April 2006 I quit my job at *CIO*, set up shop at a makeshift desk in our bedroom, and began working on the book full-time. It was the first time in my life I was not drawing a full-time paycheck and didn't have a job to return to. I was fifty-three years old and had no idea what lay around the corner. There was no guarantee my book would be published, and even if it was, that I would land another job in journalism at my age. I had taken an enormous leap of faith. And it felt completely right.

After one more trip to New York City in May to interview Rose and her colleagues again, I settled into a rhythm—reporting and writing for four to five hours and then being available when the boys came home from school. David, who was in his junior year at high school and on the tennis team, didn't come home till late, but Jake, who was still in middle school, would usually drift in around 3 pm. And I was there to talk to him and drive him to the Newton library or wherever he wanted to go.

In the fall of 2006, I jumped at the opportunity to teach a journalism class at my alma mater, Brandeis University, which was located in Waltham, a five-minute drive from my house. (By then my Adjunct teaching gig at BU had ended.) Strolling through campus every week immersed me in nostalgia; I had loved going to Brandeis as an undergraduate and while there were a few new buildings on campus, not all that much had changed.

By then, I had also applied for an Alicia Patterson Fellowship. To my amazement, I was named a finalist, and in early December, the Foundation paid for me to travel to Washington, D.C. to tell the judges in person why I needed this fellowship and how it would benefit the greater good. I thought I had a good case. While I had made good headway in gathering material for my book, a fellowship would give me the breathing room I needed to spend another year crafting the narrative and make it as compelling as possible. As I told the four judges, all of them fellow journalists like myself, I hoped my book would attract a wide readership interested in a gripping tale: how two women, Rose Firestein and Donna Howard, had exposed the deception behind the making of a bestselling drug. At the same time, I wanted my book to alert readers to the ways in which the pharmaceutical industry manipulated science to make profits. But I needed more time to report out the story. At that point, Brown University was still stonewalling my requests for information about Martin Keller and study 329 and I knew I had to reach out to other researchers involved in the clinical trial so I could connect all the dots. I also hadn't had a chance to interview in person David Healy, a British medical researcher who had been among the first doctors to write about the serious side effects of the SSRIs and whom Firestein had turned to for guidance in building her case against GlaxoSmithKline.

Near the end of 2006, I got wonderful news: I had won one of the coveted Alicia Patterson fellowships for 2007! That meant I didn't have to go out and find another job while trying to finish my book. I could focus exclusively on finishing my reporting and honing the narrative—to make it as readable as possible. I couldn't have been happier.

Sometime that year, I met with David Healy in a restaurant in downtown Boston, where he was attending a medical conference. Healy, a lanky Irishman with a Beatles haircut, gave me valuable insights into how the researchers doing study 329 had tried to twist the data to make Paxil look safer and more effective. He also shared with me his account of when he first met Firestein in July 2003 in the lobby of the Metropolitan Hostel in mid-town Manhattan. Even though Firestein had told me she would be toting a cane, Healy had to mask his surprise at seeing a small, slightly stooped woman walk haltingly into the lobby with her trademark white cane.

"She was a bit different from what you'd expect," Healy recalled with typical British understatement. "You don't expect a person who is five foot zero and has to struggle with blindness to cause such problems for a major pharmaceutical company."

Healy also told me how Rose had discovered what became the "smoking gun" in the lawsuit: an internal Glaxo memo in which corporate officials admitted that even though they knew study 329 did not show that Paxil was safe and effective in treating adolescents, they planned to market it as a positive finding to American doctors. The memo's authors had written: "It would be commercially unacceptable to include a statement that efficacy had not been demonstrated, as this would undermine the profile of paroxetine" (the generic name for Paxil). The memo proved the company's intent to deceive, and it was central to Rose's success in bringing GlaxoSmithKline to the settlement table.

How did Healy know about this memo? He explained that a whistleblower had leaked the internal memo to a BBC reporter who was doing a documentary on Paxil and that reporter, in turn, showed it to Healy, who then gave a copy of it to the *Canadian Medical Association Journal.* In the spring of 2004, the Canadian journal published an article that highlighted the smoking gun memo. (It had not been included in the first round of documents that Glaxo sent to the New York State Attorney General's office and if Healy hadn't tipped Rose off to its existence, she might never have known about it.)

Up to that point, I had not yet reached out to executives at GlaxoSmithKline. I hadn't wanted to alert them too far ahead of time that I was writing this book because I was afraid they would slap a nuisance suit on me or my publisher. Such SLAPP suits were not as common as they are now, but every investigative writer fears them, if only because they take up so much money to defend (which publishing houses, small newspapers, and book authors don't have.) I even consulted with a lawyer friend, who suggested I change the deed to our house in Newton so that if Big Pharma did sue me at some point, we wouldn't lose the house. I took his advice and changed the deed.

When I finally requested an interview with Glaxo executives, the PR spokeswoman demanded a list of questions first. And while she eventually answered some of my questions via email, I was never allowed to speak to any company executives in the course of writing the book. I did get to interview by phone one of the attorneys who represented Glaxo in the New York State Attorney General's case, but he had little to say other than a few words of grudging admiration for Rose Firestein's legal acumen.

In the spring of 2007, I took my Brandeis journalism class on a tour of the *Boston Globe*. I had arranged it with Marty Baron, the *Globe*'s new editor whom I had met when I invited him to come and talk to my graduate students at BU a year after he arrived in Boston. Baron and I hit it off and at one point, he even suggested I consider coming back to the *Globe* as a reporter. By then, however, I was working on my book proposal and wanted to see where that went first.

That spring, when I took my students on a tour of the paper, I felt like I was the prodigal daughter returning home after years away. Everyone recognized me and gave me big hugs and hellos. Jim, one of the photographers who worked the news photo desk, said I looked even younger than when I had left in 2000. But while I may not have changed much, the *Globe* felt palpably different. There were many more empty desks around the newsroom, which was much more subdued than I remembered. My students and I were invited to sit in on the afternoon editorial meeting, but the mood felt somber, even sour. The only person who did much talking during the meeting was Marty. Someone made a lame joke about a bloody sock, something to do with whether Kurt Schilling's sock had been doctored. As I remembered it, there had been a lot more energy and jokes in the few news meetings I had attended while working at the paper in the nineties. As we walked out of the meeting, I felt like I was standing on the deck of the Titanic. Internet companies like Google, Facebook, and Craigslist had begun sucking up the advertising dollars that had once made newspapers so profitable, and like so many other metropolitan papers, the *Globe*'s staff had shrunk accordingly. Even my students commented on the funereal mood in the newsroom as we drove back to campus. And that's when it hit me, like a blast of cold air: Even though I had been devastated by the *Globe*'s treatment of me in 2000, Fiona had done me a favor, by pushing me out the door. The *Boston Globe* was no longer the vibrant newspaper I knew and loved. The visit with my students, I realized, had given me a gratifying sense of closure.

By the summer of 2007, I was racing to finish a first draft of the book. Even so, I took a break in late August so we could take our son, David, to Lewisburg, PA, where he was slated to start his freshman year at Bucknell University. The previous summer, my husband and I had taken turns squiring David around to a number of liberal arts colleges in New England and Pennsylvania, and while he turned his nose up at Vassar and Wesleyan—they were too artsy fartsy, he said—he had fallen in love with Bucknell. That weekend, we left our fifteen-year-old son, Jake, in the care of his paternal grandfather who had come down from New Hampshire to stay at our house and squire Jake to a soccer game that Sunday.

I was teary-eyed by the time we unpacked David's belongings in his dorm and it was time to say goodbye. I couldn't believe my little boy had grown up so quickly. Where had the years gone? David was eager to meet his new roommates and explore the campus so we didn't linger. He gave us a quick hug and we drove away, tears clogging my sinuses.

We were halfway home when we got the call. Jake had been kicked in the balls during the soccer game and one of his testicles had swollen to the size of a grapefruit. Grandpa had taken him to the local ER, where they iced his testicles and assured him the swelling would go down. My husband and I raced home, breaking a few speed limits, to find Jake resting comfortably and playing cards with Grandpa. The swelling did go down and Jake was back to playing soccer within the week. Several weeks later, we got a bill for more than $2,000 for that fifteen-minute visit to the ER. I fought the charges and eventually got the doctor who had treated Jake to reduce his fee, but we still paid a hefty amount for our son's visit to the ER that afternoon.

By October, I had finished a draft of my book and sent it off to my editor at Algonquin, a warm, wise woman by the name of Amy Gash. I also emailed Jonathan Albano, the lawyer with whom I had worked at the *Boston Globe* on several investigative pieces and asked him if he would mind taking a look at my manuscript and make sure I had written nothing that could be construed as libelous. I told Albano that I would be happy to pay him for his time. He promptly replied that he would be delighted to take a look and would charge me nothing for the service. Albano must have known that investigative writers are almost always writing on a shoestring, but I will never forget his generosity. I also suggested that Algonquin have their own in-house lawyer look over the manuscript.

Albano and the in-house lawyer suggested a few minor tweaks but both felt the book was on solid ground and could withstand any legal grenades the pharmaceutical industry might throw at it. Amy weighed in with a number of other suggested edits and questions. Even so, I was able to turn the revisions around by early 2008.

In the meantime, I had started looking for a full-time teaching job that would allow me to teach a few classes, earn a living, and continue writing books. I was still teaching one journalism course each semester at Brandeis University, but the journalism program there couldn't afford another full-time professor. And I knew I couldn't make a living from writing books. The publishing industry was already being pummeled by Amazon's price undercutting, and the kind of books I was interested in writing—investigative nonfiction—were not going to provide sufficient remuneration for my family and I to live on. Lucky for me, Steve Whitfield, the chair of the American Studies Department who oversaw the journalism program at Brandeis, happened to know the professor who oversaw the journalism program at Mount Holyoke College, a women's college in Western Massachusetts. And even more coincidentally, Mount Holyoke had an opening for a full-time journalism professor in its writing program. Steve's letter of recommendation was enough to get me an interview there. Having a nonfiction book about the pharmaceutical industry about to be released in a few months didn't hurt either. In mid-March, I received the welcome news that Mount Holyoke had hired me as a full-time visiting professor of journalism, beginning in the fall of 2008. My gamble—in leaving a stable job at *CIO* magazine to write a book—had paid off. Or so it seemed.

My book, which the publishers had titled *Side Effects: A Prosecutor, a Whistleblower and a Bestselling Antidepressant on Trial*, was just about to hit the presses when a bombshell hit. Eliot Spitzer, by then governor of New York, was caught sending thousands of dollars electronically to a high-class escort. Federal investigators had been tipped off to the money transfer by one of the Wall Street banks that Spitzer had gone after for financial conflicts of interest as the state's attorney general. The Department of Justice under George W. Bush threatened to bring criminal charges against him for patronizing a prostitute unless he resigned as governor. At the time, Spitzer, who was a very popular governor, was being touted as a possible Democratic presidential candidate. The Bush administration was playing political hardball and it worked. Spitzer chose to step down as governor in March 2008 and the DOJ never brought any charges against him.

I called my editor in a panic—did we have time to update my description of Spitzer in the final pages of my book? The answer was yes and I dashed off a few new sentences, which made it into the book just before it hit the presses.

I breathed a sigh of relief, and then I waited for whatever dust devil might erupt when *Side Effects* was released. Its scheduled publication date was June 17, 2008.

Chapter 21

THE WEEK MY book was released, I gave an evening talk at Harvard Bookstore in Cambridge, Massachusetts. Friends and former colleagues from the *Boston Globe* came to hear what I had to say, along with people attracted by the subject matter and a few patrons who happened to be browsing through the bookstore that evening. I was wearing my power outfit, a tailored peach jacket over a short-sleeved black top and black pants, and I stood behind a podium in front of forty or fifty people sitting on folding chairs. As a one-time theater nut who had taken acting classes in high school, I had no problems getting up in front of an audience. But I was always nervous beforehand. It was only after I began talking—with my notes in front of me—that the jitters went away.

As I had done at my first book talk at Newtonville Books a few nights prior, I started out by asking the crowd, "How many of you are taking prescription drugs? Can I see a show of hands?" Quite a few people raised their hands. And then I asked, "How many of you have been prescribed drugs and not told about the harmful side effects of the drugs you are taking?" A handful of hands shot in the air.

At that point, a hefty woman with tangled hair stood up in the front row, turned her back to me, and pointed to some writing on her T-shirt. A list appeared to be scrawled in large black magic marker on her shirt, but the only words I could make out were "DMH." I could feel my face flush with nervous embarrassment; this woman could disrupt the entire evening if I didn't handle things right. There were a few titters from the audience but I didn't join them. I walked around the podium and tried to read the writing on her T-shirt.

"Sounds like you have some grievances against the Massachusetts Department of Mental Health," I said in as soothing a tone I could muster. "Sorry to hear they've been giving you a hard time. I appreciate your sharing this with us."

The woman turned around and smiled at me gratefully. And then to my enormous relief, she sat back down, and I was able to proceed. After I gave my prepared spiel, I read a passage from the book about a scary visit that Donna Howard had received from federal agents at her home after she blew the whistle on Marty Keller and Brown. The excerpt began:

> It was dark by the time Donna Howard pulled into her driveway, but she could see the black Lincoln Continental parked on the side of the road, an anomaly in her working-class neighborhood of beat-up pickup trucks. She knew the two men sitting inside the car were federal agents because one of them had called her earlier that day at the hospital. He said he was from the U.S. Postal Service, investigating the possibility of mail fraud. Howard didn't quite know what meant, and she was afraid to ask. The man sounded friendly enough. Could he drop by this evening to talk to her? Aghast that a law enforcement agent had called her at work—how did he know her number, anyway?— Donna tried to quell the queasiness surging up her throat. This was the last thing she needed right now. Thinking fast, Howard told him she had to take her daughter for a doctor's appointment and wouldn't be home until after 7 pm. "That's okay," the agent said. "We don't mind the late hour."

After I finished the excerpt, I opened the event up to questions. Fortunately, the woman with the marked-up T-shirt had already wandered off. Charlie, one of my friends from the *Globe*, was sitting in the front row. "What I'd like to know is: Weren't you worried the pharmaceutical industry was going to come after you because of what you wrote?" he asked. Charlie had been a long-time business reporter at the *Globe*; he was now a reporter at Bloomberg News.

I laughed. "Yes, I was. I was afraid they would hit me with a lawsuit—you know, to intimidate me. I even changed the deed to our house to make sure I wouldn't lose it in any legal action. But as I tell my students, truth is the best defense against libel and I knew I was telling the truth. Of course, I made sure to have a libel lawyer look over the manuscript."

"So has anyone sued you?" Charlie asked.

"Not yet," I said. The audience laughed and I moved on to the next question.

I ended up giving talks at four bookstores in Massachusetts and three in the Philadelphia area that summer. My mom, bless her heart, had printed up colorful postcards, which she distributed to all her friends and neighbors, announcing that "our daughter, Alison Bass, will be discussing her new book, *Side Effects: A Prosecutor, a Whistleblower and a Bestselling Antidepressant on Trial*," at two local venues in June. Mom had always wanted to be a published author. She had even written two novels but had been unable to get them published. Yet she never evinced any jealousy or resentment that I had accomplished something she had yet to. Instead she was my biggest fan. She even wrote a letter to John Stewart, then the host of the *Daily Show*, extolling my book's virtues and telling him he should invite me on his show. She was disappointed that Stewart never wrote back to her.

"We don't watch the *Daily Show* anymore," she told me that summer. "He should have had the courtesy to write back."

Mom's friends were more loyal. At least thirty of them turned up at the talk I gave at Doylestown Bookshop on June 23. A few of my old high school classmates showed up as well, as did David, my brother-in-law's younger brother, whom I had taken to my senior prom in high school. David was now a highly successful pediatric dentist (with three offices) and it warmed me inside that he had taken the time to come to my talk.

"I'm proud of you Alison," he said and gave me a big hug.

I knew bookstore appearances were important to selling my book, if only because the stores would not only stock the books but would put them out front to entice readers. Even more important were the reviews and media interviews. I had hoped the *New York Times Sunday Book Review*, which was considered the holy grail for authors because of its wide circulation, would publish a review of the book. But it never did, which was a huge disappointment. However, I got a lot of positive press from others, including the *New York Review of Books*, a smaller, more literary publication than the *Times*, *USA Today*, the *Boston Globe*, *Associated Press*, *Raleigh News and Observer*, the *Bucks County Courier Times*, the *Doylestown Intelligencer*, and the *New England Journal of Medicine*, among other papers, magazines and news sites. One influential blogger wrote:

> *Side Effects* reads like a John Grisham thriller, but it teaches you everything you need to know about how some drug companies have used their marketing and legal muscle to lie about science.

There were only two negative reviews of my book and not surprisingly, they came from people who had been on the pharmaceutical industry's payroll. A lawyer who defended drug companies in wrongful injury lawsuits panned my book in the pages of the *Wall Street Journal*. The *Journal* violated a core journalistic principle of nonpartisanship in allowing a drug company insider to write the review, but at least the paper disclosed his conflict of interest at the end. Not so the *Philadelphia Inquirer*. That newspaper allowed a researcher who had been a consultant for GlaxoSmithKline, to write a review, which was negative. "The investigative reporting and legal spadework [in this book] are pretty pedestrian," the reviewer concluded.

That review stung, but what bothered me most was that there was no disclosure of the reviewer's conflict of interest—in having consulted for Glaxo. I wrote an angry letter to the editor about that omission, which the paper never published. I felt like I was on a roller coaster, soaring with every good review, plummeting with each bad one. I finally understood why actors don't read reviews of their work; they're just too painful, even the positive ones. With the publication of my book, I felt as though I was baring my soul to the world.

That July, I was scheduled to give a talk at Bunch of Grapes, a popular bookstore on Martha's Vineyard that attracted many summer visitors to its talks. Mom had fallen in love with the Vineyard almost forty years prior when she began hosteling on the island, bringing along whichever of her children were available at the time. The island's lone hostel was located in West Tisbury, which had an unusually restrictive policy then: it only allowed people who arrived by bike or on foot to stay as guests. We had to bike from the ferry in Vineyard Haven about ten miles just to get to the hostel. We cycled all over the island, including to the fishing port at Menemsha, where my mother would purchase a bunch of live lobsters and throw them in our saddlebags for the seven-mile bike trip back to the hostel. I always managed to avoid being in the kitchen when the time came to boil them. But I had to admit I loved eating the cooked product. In 1972, when my parents were going through a rough patch in their marriage, Mom convinced my dad to purchase a small two-bedroom Cape in Edgartown for $35,000. Over the years, as their children got married and started having kids themselves, they enlarged the house to four bedrooms, three bathrooms, a spacious living area, a separate dining room and an attic that could sleep up to four little ones. We all visited with our respective families at some point during the summer and often overlapped with each other so our kids could play with their cousins. Since I lived in the Boston area, an easy one-and-a-half hour drive to Woods Hole, where the ferry to Martha's Vineyard docked, my family and I spent the most time on the Vineyard, coming down on weekends (when there were no soccer tournaments) and during our summer vacations. In the summer of 2008, it made sense to arrange a book talk on the island since I would be there for vacation anyway.

But a few weeks before my scheduled book talk in late July, the Bunch of Grapes burnt down. All book talks were cancelled and rebuilding the store would take years. Edgartown Books on Main Street did not host talks, nor did the town library, which at that time inhabited a cramped space a few blocks away. So I hastily re-arranged my talk at the spanking new West Tisbury public library.

That afternoon, as I stood at the podium looking out over the audience, I realized it was comprised mostly of my family. There were only four strangers present, along with twelve members of my own extended family. I made a joke about this being a family affair and how I was probably more nervous this afternoon than I had been before my other talks, because my two brothers and their families were sitting right in front of me, along with my two sons, my parents, and my husband.

"We promise we won't heckle you," yelled one of my nephews, being his usual smart-aleck self.

Everyone laughed. Afterward, another nephew, who was a senior in college, came up to me and said, "Interesting talk! I had no idea the pharmaceutical industry was so corrupt. Good thing I'm not planning to be a doctor." His father, my brother, was a doctor, but thankfully he didn't overhear Dan's remark.

After the talk, we all drove to the quaint fishing village of Menemsha so Mom could buy some fresh fish for dinner that night. As she shopped in Larsen's market, the rest of us strolled around, admiring the sailboats anchored in the harbor. We walked down the pier that jutted out alongside the narrow entrance to the harbor, and I took off my shoes and waded into the sea. In a picture one of my brothers took as we sat on the rocks by the pier, I look happy and relaxed, still dressed in my black top and black capri pants, my bare feet sandy. I had reason to be content; my duties for the day were done and I was surrounded by the people I loved most in the world.

Chapter 22

ON A MILD September evening in 2009, I drove to a restaurant in Springfield, Massachusetts to meet a sex worker I had spoken to once on the phone. Elle St. Claire had contacted me after another sex worker spread the word on a private listserv that I was interested in writing about the sex industry. Before meeting her, I had perused Elle's website, which featured photos of her posing seductively in various states of undress. She was a beauty, tall with long toned legs and shoulder-length blond hair.

That evening, when I got out of my car and started walking toward the restaurant, I noticed a tall, red-haired woman wearing high heels and a sleeveless black dress with spaghetti straps. Walking next to her was a much shorter, curvier woman with cascading blond hair. That must be Elle and her wife, I thought, and picked up my pace. But then I stopped short and my mouth dropped open. Elle was or had been a man. Her shoulders were much too broad to belong to a woman. I froze. On her website, I had seen no evidence that she was transgender. True, the photos were a bit fuzzy but I saw nothing on the site to indicate Elle's true gender identity. Perhaps I just hadn't looked close enough. This was going to be interesting. I took a deep breath and walked into the restaurant.

I hadn't given much thought to the largely hidden world of sex work until a few months ago when a student of mine at Mount Holyoke College met with me to go over a profile that she had written for a class assignment. She had chosen to write about a young activist who helped defeat an ordinance that would have made it illegal for homeless people to panhandle on the streets of Northampton, a progressive but increasingly gentrified city in western Massachusetts. My student had heard this young woman speak at a town meeting and was impressed by her passion for helping those less fortunate than herself. But the student was having trouble bringing her subject to life on the page, and as we discussed how to do that, she suddenly blurted out, "She's a sex worker, you know." How fascinating, I thought. Two other facts leaped out at me: the activist's middle-class background and the fact she came from an Orthodox Jewish family. The student didn't end up mentioning what this woman did for a living in her profile, but I was curious about her since she seemed to defy every stereotype I had about prostitutes.

Jillian (her work name) agreed to meet me in one of those hip cafés that line the Main Street of Northampton. She arrived at the café a few minutes late, dressed entirely in black: a low-cut black top, a long black skirt and a black leather jacket adorned with a button that said Activist. Her long hair was jet black and she had freckles across her nose. I was immediately struck by how articulate and well-educated Jillian was. Although she had dropped out of college, she was widely read and had informed opinions on capitalism, the psychiatric establishment, the sociopolitical structure of the U.S., you name it. During our chat, the topic of how this twenty-seven-year-old earned a living came up.

"I enjoy being a middle-class escort," she said, as if what she did was just another ordinary job. "I provide a girlfriend experience for an hour. It's fun."

The stories that Jillian told me about her work clashed with the popular narrative of all prostitutes being drug-addicted, victimized women who are forced into the sex trade by abusive pimps and traffickers. According to Jillian, most adult sex workers in the U.S., including streetwalkers, were selling sex by choice, primarily for economic reasons. Laws that criminalized prostitution, she said, only made it harder for sex workers to protect themselves from physical violence and sexually transmitted diseases. I was eager to hear more. I had always been drawn to reporting on marginalized communities and exposing fallacies about them; that's one of the reasons I covered mental health for the *Boston Globe* for so long. Much of my career involved reporting about victims of sexual abuse and exploitation as they searched for justice, so writing about sex workers seemed to be a natural extension of this lifelong vocation.

When I expressed an interest in writing about her profession, Jillian promised to put me in touch with some of her colleagues. One of the first to reach out to me was Elle. On the phone, she had a husky voice and said she'd be happy to meet me for drinks.

"My wife will come too," she said. "We could just sit and talk; I have a lot of questions for you."

When I caught up with Elle and her wife inside the restaurant—they were standing at the *maître d'* station—my suspicions were confirmed. Elle had muscular upper arms and an angular form that tapered to a narrow waist. Her companion was much curvier with an angelic-looking face framed by blond curly ringlets. When I approached, they were talking to a man in a dark suit who looked distinctly uncomfortable.

"Hi, I'm Alison Bass and you're Elle, I presume," I said and shot an amiable smile at the *maître d'*. "We're here for dinner. Do you have a table for three?"

Although Elle had earlier mentioned her wife, she introduced her companion to me as "Jessica, she's my fiancé." We shook hands all around and the *maître d'*, still looking nonplussed, escorted us upstairs. At first he steered us to a table set well away from the other diners under a loud TV near the bar.

I gave him an imploring smile.

"I'm here to interview Elle and Jessica and it's too noisy here," I said. "Would you mind seating us somewhere else? Maybe a booth?"

The *maître d'* was clearly not happy. He looked the three of us over again and then reached a decision. This wasn't worth a scene. "Okay," he said and led us over to a corner booth by some large plate-glass windows. As we settled ourselves, I noticed that the people in the booth behind us were staring. Elle and Jessica must get this treatment all the time, I thought, and felt a rush of anger at the other diners' rudeness.

As if she read my mind, Elle shrugged. "This happens all the time when we go out. That's why we don't go out in public a lot."

I nodded sympathetically. Elle wanted to hear about me and my career and we engaged in small talk while perusing the menu. When I asked her if Elle St. Claire was her real name, she laughed. "No that's my nom de plume," she said. We ordered some food and Elle and Jessica both ordered cocktails while I stuck with water. And then I dispensed with the chit-chat.

"I thought you were a woman," I said. "You sure look like one on your website."

Elle giggled, a high-pitched oddly discordant rasp that contrasted with her deeper speaking voice. "I make that clear on my website. I also put it in the ad. Sometimes people show up and say they didn't know. If they're not comfortable with that, I make light of it and say I'm not offended. I say, 'If you're interested in a woman, you can see Jessica.'"

As it turned out, both Jessica and Elle did sex work. They also performed in live web cams and erotic porn. Elle also danced in live adult shows and she did phone sex as well.

"I can be sitting around and working on the phone and cam, while I wait for the next [escort] call," Elle said. She explained that she and Jessica worked out of their home, a three-story rental duplex in Holyoke. They lived on the ground floor, recorded the live web cam performances on the second floor and met with clients on the third floor, which was reachable by a separate entrance and staircase.

As we talked, I scribbled notes into my notebook and now and then forked a bite to eat. We talked for hours that evening and later that fall and the following year, I visited Elle and Jessica several times at their white-shingled home in Holyoke. I felt strangely drawn to Elle. She was articulate and charismatic, even though she chain-smoked Marlboro cigarettes as we chatted. She was the first transgender woman I had ever met and I found her life story fascinating.

Elle had been born male in a working-class household in Massachusetts. Her father, a first generation Irish American, served in the Korean War and drank to excess. Her parents divorced when she was eight and her mother eventually remarried. Elle went to an all-boys Catholic school, where she became captain of the football team and class president. She was also a gifted dancer and musician (she played the saxophone) and in her senior year she was accepted into the Berklee College of Music in Boston. But her stepfather refused to sign a waiver so that she could obtain financial aid to attend Berklee. Instead, she decided to tour with the popular singing and dancing troupe Up with People. It was while she was on a world tour with Up with People that she got an inkling of her true identity.

"We were walking around the red-light district in Amsterdam and we knocked on some doors and I went in [one window unit]," Elle recalled. "And it was like, wow. The penis was flopping around and the tits were flapping. When I saw my first transsexual in Amsterdam, my first reaction was that it was so hot, and then I realized I'm not sexually attracted to this person. I am this person."

It took Elle several years to find the courage to come out of the closet. In the meantime, she married, became a real estate broker, and fathered two sons. When she finally told her wife who she really was, her wife kicked her out of the house and told everyone that her husband was transsexual, ruining Elle's career in real estate.

"Within twelve hours, I found that the life I had built was gone," Elle said. She changed her name legally to a woman's name and began driving a cab. Nine months later, she received custody of her two boys after their mother had a nervous breakdown and was confined to a psychiatric hospital.

In addition to spending time with Jillian, Elle, and several other sex workers, I did some research. And what I found jibed with what they had been telling me: that the vast majority of men and women selling sex in the United States were doing so by choice. Jillian and Elle were the first to admit there was exploitation in the sex industry and that some people, mostly teenage girls, were being coerced into the trade by abusive pimps or traffickers. Indeed, under federal law, anyone under the age of eighteen who sells sex is considered a trafficking victim. But as I discovered, the number of women and children purportedly being trafficked in the U.S. had been grossly exaggerated by advocacy groups who were conflating consensual prostitution with sex trafficking. Furthermore, studies by respected scholars showed that laws criminalizing prostitution were not only largely ineffective in curbing the sex trade, but were creating an atmosphere that encouraged the exploitation of sex workers and violence against all women. Studies also showed that anti-prostitution laws only made it more difficult for sex workers to protect themselves—from physical harm and from sexually transmitted diseases such as HIV.

Between the research and the rich stories of the sex workers I'd interviewed, I thought I had some great material for a book. But my agent and editor at Algonquin (who had first dibs on my next book) disagreed.

"Who's going to read this book?" asked Amy Gash, my editor at Algonquin. "Women aren't going to be interested because they don't want to think of their husbands patronizing a prostitute. And men aren't going to be caught dead with the book for fear of what their wives or girlfriends will think."

Nor was Amy impressed with the stories I had collected of individual sex workers. "They're kind of depressing don't you think?"

I didn't think so. I thought some of the stories I had collected were uplifting and transformative. And I was outraged by the fact that sex workers, already stigmatized by society for what they did, were getting arrested and harassed every day because of criminal laws that seemed ineffectual and unjust. No one else seemed to be writing about this issue and I was eager to expose widespread misinformation about sex work, to correct the record so to speak. Research done in other countries indicated that legalizing sex work led to reductions in both physical violence and rates of HIV. As far as I could see, decriminalizing sex work was analogous to legalizing marijuana. It would not only eliminate the criminal underbelly of the trade but would make life safer for sex workers, their families, and their clients.

After Algonquin and my agent passed on the project, I sent my book proposal to a number of other agents. But they were similarly indifferent. In the meantime, I got some good news: a staff investigator for Senator Charles Grassley (R-Iowa) called to tell me he had read *Side Effects* and was using it "as a template" in investigating psychiatric researchers who, like Keller, had failed to disclose their financial ties to the pharmaceutical industry. Grassley held a number of hearings on this issue and began pushing for legislation that would require pharm companies to publicly disclose money they gave to doctors and other health-care professionals to promote their drugs. The staff investigator told me he had bought a bunch of my books and was passing them out to key players on Capitol Hill.

"Hey thanks, Paul, that's really nice of you," I said.

"Yup," he replied. "It's a good book."

When the Affordable Care Act was passed in March 2010, it contained the Physician Payment Sunshine Act, which required drug companies to publicly disclose payments they made to physicians for consulting, speaking, and other personal fees. Grassley had insisted on its insertion before mobilizing bipartisan support for the ACA.

I didn't find an agent for my sex work book until the fall of 2011. Russ, who was a partner in a New York literary agency, had responded to my query with a lengthy email critiquing my proposal. When I spoke to him by phone, Russ said he had been approached by a madam who ran several brothels in mid-town Manhattan and had an amazing life story.

"Julie had to go into the witness protection program at one point because she was going to testify against some murdering pimps. Her story might be just what you need to sell your book," Russ said. "I think you should meet her. Interested?"

I was.

Chapter 23

IN JANUARY 2011, I met Julie Moya at Russ's condo on the Upper West Side of Manhattan. The woman the *New York Post* had once called a "notorious madam" arrived toting a shopping bag that contained several yellowed clippings of articles about her life as a high-end escort in the 1980s. When I met Julie, she was fifty-three, short and plump, with beautiful slanted green eyes, a slightly crooked nose, and shoulder-length blond hair. She wore a high-necked black ruffled blouse and black skirt and looked more like the principal of a private Catholic school than a notorious madam. Her clippings, however, revealed a different story. In one clip, which featured her on the cover of *NYC Adult Today* (a now defunct magazine), a much younger Julie is hoisting a glass of bubbly, her ample cleavage spilling over a low-cut dress. She looks clearly delighted to be part of the Big Apple party scene.

Between bites of dim sum, Julie told me her story. She had been born in Cincinnati, Ohio, to an unmarried sixteen-year-old; she never knew her biological father. Her mother eventually married a man who didn't much like Julie. He and her mother had four more children and Julie said she always felt like an outsider, starved for attention. She dropped out of school and got married at the age of thirteen after the nineteen-year-old man she had been seeing got her pregnant. He soon left her, and Julie, still living at home, gave birth at the age of fourteen to a little girl with a serious heart defect.

"I remember standing over her crib one day, she was a blue baby, struggling to breathe and I thought I should put her out of misery, I should end her life," Julie said, speaking in a low husky voice. "I knew I had to get out of there. So I ran away."

She bounced from friend to friend, living on the streets for a while and ended up in a homeless shelter for teens. At the age of fifteen, she started doing erotic dancing at a local nightclub.

"I was dancing for the Hustler Club on Walnut Street; Larry Flynt owned it," she said. When I asked if people at the club knew her age, she said yes. "They didn't care."

Julie said she started selling sex when she was sixteen, mostly to older men who were friends of Larry Flynt. While she was working at the Hustler Club, she was also asked to give out cards advertising a brothel just over the border in Kentucky.

"It was called a lockup because they didn't allow the girls to leave for a few days," she said. "They murdered a couple of girls there and the FBI started looking into it."

When the FBI swooped in, Julie, then nineteen, was arrested for promoting prostitution. She agreed to cooperate with the FBI men in exchange for getting into the witness protection program. I was moved and intrigued by Julie's story and wanted to know more. But I sensed that she was not comfortable with telling Russ and me the whole story of how she ended up in the witness protection program. So I didn't probe. But Russ had no such compunctions. He kept asking her questions until she said, "I testified against the men who were accused of murdering the girls." And then she clammed up.

I changed the topic and shot Russ a look that meant back off, let her talk at her own pace. He was asking her even more questions than I, the presumed reporter, was. Yet Julie didn't get angry or flustered. She remained pleasant, even deferential to Russ. I could see why she would be a good madam—she knew how to manage men.

By the time we said our goodbyes, it was clear to me that Julie Moya's story would be an important one to tell, in no small part because she had overcome such adversity. There were so many interesting threads to her life: how she ended up in New York selling sex as a high-end escort, had two more children, both boys, and got married to a drug dealer from Argentina. She even went to live with her new husband in Argentina for a year but didn't like the way that men in Mendoza treated women. Shortly after she came back to New York and got divorced, she opened a brothel on the Upper East Side that catered to professional athletes, Wall Street types, and anyone who could afford to pay $300 to $600 an hour for her girls. This was in the mid-nineties, and as she proudly told us that evening, "My place was cited as Best GFE [girlfriend experience] on JAG, this website where men exchange notes about [their encounters]."

A few weeks later, I interviewed Julie Moya again by phone to get some further details about her life for the book proposal I was revising. And then in July 2011, I took the train back to New York to spend more time with Julie. We arranged to meet at a restaurant in Tribeca, because that was close to my niece's condo, where I was staying overnight. When she rushed in fifteen minutes late, I could see that she had lost weight. She looked younger and more polished than she had in January, dressed all in black, her blond hair a shoulder-length page-boy.

"I'm so sorry I'm late," she said and gave me a big hug. "I had to deal with this situation with my grandson." A friend, she said, had driven her in from Long Island and dropped her off at the restaurant.

When we sat down in a back booth, Moya explained that her five-year-old grandson had been removed from his father's house by New York's child protective services. The boy's father, Julie's son, helped manage her brothels. Her grandson was currently staying with relatives on Long Island and Moya visited him every day.

"[My grandson] was saying some strange things. Apparently, my son was letting him touch his girlfriend's breasts. I took him to a psychiatrist and she called ACS [child protection services]," Moya said. "My son thinks it's funny but it's not funny at all. My grandson is having nightmares."

Moya ordered some soup and I a corned beef sandwich with pickles. When I asked her why she had chosen to become a sex worker, she said because she liked the money and she liked the attention. "I like pleasing people." She paused for a moment and then added, "Many girls in the business had a sexual molestation experience when they were young. I see prostitution as a way of getting back control over your own body."

Moya was trying to tell me something so I asked the obvious question: Had she ever been molested as a child?

"I was molested by a relative when I was ten," she said. "I would sit in his lap and he would feel me up and he wanted me to touch his ... It was just hands. It went on for months. But I liked it, the attention and stuff. It was an uncle. I finally told my grandmother and she said don't ever go near him again."

I felt a rush of compassion for the woman sitting across from me. She had had a very tough life and yet she seemed to have done the best she could with the hand she had been dealt. Julie was a survivor, and I felt a kinship with her.

As we ate, Julie told me more about her childhood and how she ended up in the witness protection program. After she was arrested, she said the men who owned the Kentucky lockup sent a correctional officer to warn her to keep her mouth shut or else. She was terrified. She confided in her mother, who hired a lawyer. The next thing Julie knew, the FBI had taken her out of jail, put her up at a local hotel, and begun questioning her. But the interrogation was only part of it.

"The FBI guy came onto me sexually when he was interviewing me," she said. "He would come behind me and grab my breasts." One of the Marshalls who guarded Julie reported the abusive FBI agent and he was reassigned. Julie eventually testified against the pimps who ran the lockdown in a trial that was covered by the Cincinnati papers. She was then relocated to another city and given a new identity and a job at a local department store.

When I had talked to Julie on the phone about coming down to New York again, she had said she would try to show me one of her brothels in mid-town. Her promise made me apprehensive and excited at the same time. The journalist in me knew that a first-hand description of an illegal brothel in Manhattan would add texture to my book, but what if police raided the place while I was there? Would I be carted to the station in a paddy wagon along with the rest of the women?

After Julie and I finished eating that evening in Tribeca, we walked over to Eighth Avenue and she hailed a taxi. She instructed the driver to take us to 44th street between 8th and 9th Avenues. In the cab, I told her a little bit about my husband and sons and asked her if she was in a relationship.

"I'm not interested in a relationship with a man," she replied. "If anything, I would have a relationship with a woman—as a companion."

I looked down at my notebook, trying to hide the surprised expression on my face. Was this fifty-three-year-old madam coming on to me? Or was she just being completely honest?

When we arrived at our destination, a nondescript brownstone midway down 44th Street, Julie pressed the front door bell and spoke into the intercom. The door buzzed open and we walked up to an apartment on the second floor. On the way up, Julie had explained we were visiting her smallest brothel, where she tried out new sex workers to see how they did. Only regular customers were allowed in.

We walked into a small kitchen and living room area, where several women milled around. One woman sat on a maroon leather couch watching *True Blood*, an HBO show about vampires, on a television mounted on the wall. Another stood in the cramped New York-style kitchen answering five or six cell phones lying on the counter. Julie introduced her as Sienna and explained that she was arranging liaisons for clients not only for this location but the other brothels as well.

"Some of the men calling are regulars; they ask for specific girls. Some say who do you recommend? Who's on tonight?" said Sienna, who had long dark hair, brown eyes, and a businesslike air. She said she used to be an escort and a dominatrix but now handles the phones and does security. She was thirty-four, she said, almost thirty-five.

Sienna stopped talking to pick up another buzzing phone.

"All right. I got you down for a half-hour at nine-thirty. Call me when you get to the corner," she said into the phone. After hanging up, she called the other brothel and told them that "John" would be there shortly. She explained that she never gives the exact address to new clients until they call back and say they're at the corner. It was a security measure.

Before Julie could introduce me to more of the women, a clean-cut-looking Asian American man who looked like he was in his forties, walked into the apartment. He went directly into one of the bedrooms with "Taylor," a slim, pretty woman with long dark hair.

In between buzzing cell phones, Sienna explained that they only use cell phones at the brothels because "landlines are easier to tap."

"Occasionally we have to move places but we keep the same numbers, which is good, so regulars can find us," Sienna said. She said she used to be an executive assistant to the CEO of a nonprofit but she got laid off and couldn't find another job. She was hired by Julie just before her unemployment benefits ran out. "I needed money fast."

"When I met Julie, we just hit it off," Sienna said. "She's just amazing. She's my girlfriend. She helped me out at a dark time in my life. I was estranged from my family for two years and she helped me get back with them again."

Julie introduced me to another woman, Corrine, who had been in the bathroom when we first arrived. Corrine, who wore her brown hair in two long braids and looked like a flower child from the sixties, said she used to be an escort and exotic dancer. Now she also handled the phones.

"I'm forty-one and I figure I'm done with my career as a working girl," said Corrine, who had taught school in the Bronx before embarking on sex work. She said she handled the phones during the day and Sienna did the nights.

While Sienna was talking on one phone, Corrine picked up another one that was buzzing. I heard her say, "Honey, how long would it take you to get to 44th street and 9th?" She put a hand over the receiver and whispered, "It's Jimmy. He's a regular." She turned to Sienna. "How long is Sadie going to be here?"

"Till ten-thirty," Sienna responded.

Corrine spoke into the phone. "You can come over now. Kerry went home but Sadie will be here." She hung up just as another cell phone buzzed.

While Sienna and Corrine were busy answering calls, Julie introduced me to a young woman with a baby face and crooked teeth. Her breasts were spilling out of a low cut black lingerie slip.

"This is Sadie," Julie said. "She's new."

Sadie told me she was from Alabama and had "lived around" before that. She had come to New York with her boyfriend. She said she was nineteen and would be twenty in twenty-one days. I asked her why she had decided to do sex work.

"I need the money to fix my teeth," she said. "And you know, living in New York is very expensive."

Just then, Jimmy walked into the living room. He was Indian and dressed in a suit as if he had just come from work. Sadie greeted him and took him into the other bedroom.

A little while later, Taylor came out with her client. She was dressed in nothing but a white towel. She had a stack of bills in her hand, which she handed over to Sienna. Sienna counted it carefully and gave Taylor a tip.

I asked Julie how much she charged.

"It's $160 for a half-hour; $240 for an hour," she said. This was a special discounted rate for regulars who were trying out the "new girls," she explained. At Julie's other brothels, she charged as much as $300 an hour for some of the more popular sex workers.

"We're not real high-end," she said. "We're the Walmart of sex escorts."

At 9:25 pm, Taylor, who has just come back out of the bathroom, was told she had to see another client at nine-thirty. She looked surprised. She had no makeup on and was still wearing a white towel.

Five minutes later, a bald young man wearing a baseball cap came into the apartment. "This is your client," Sienna said to Taylor, who had quickly donned a black negligee. "Go greet him."

The two disappeared into the bedroom. Julie drew me to the couch and showed me a website called eroticareview.com. "It's a site where johns write reviews of various girls," Julie explained. "Oh, this isn't good. It's a review by a john who says Tatiana wouldn't let him touch her hair or go down on her."

A little later, Taylor came out of the bedroom to complain that the client she was with wanted to start the session over because she had spent a few minutes in the bathroom after he arrived.

"I can't do that," Taylor said. "My boyfriend is coming to pick me up at ten-thirty."

Julie looked up from her laptop, a frown on her face.

"You need to go back inside and not complain about a client when they can hear you," she said firmly. Taylor did as she was told and as soon as the bedroom door shut behind her, Sienna whispered, "She's a real prima donna. After [her client] came, she went into the bathroom for a long time. She should have done that before the session."

I felt bad about the way Taylor was being treated. She had not been given enough time to get ready for the man in the baseball cap and now she was being blamed for it. I didn't like the way Sienna was talking about her and yet I knew at some level that this kind of sniping was not unique to sex work. Employees in many occupations are often mistreated by mid-level managers trying to suck up to the boss. Indeed, I had experienced that myself at Mount Holyoke. Those of us teaching there as professional writers were treated as second-class citizens by much of the English Department faculty, who made it clear we were there only at their sufferance. We were not supposed to speak up at faculty meetings and the one time I made the mistake of saying something, I was laughed at.

"Did she really mispronounce bison?" one of the professors asked incredulously, speaking about me as if I was invisible. Her colleagues laughed and I felt thoroughly humiliated and silenced.

Later on, when I tried to suggest the college bring in more revenue by launching a summer writing program at Mount Holyoke, the then chair of the department called me "strident" and dismissed the idea. So while I felt bad for Taylor that evening in Manhattan, I understood the group dynamics that prompt people to gang up on new and possibly threatening employees. I wondered how long she would last at the brothel and why she was doing sex work in the first place. I never did find out. Julie had to leave around 10 pm to go to the other brothel and I left the apartment with her. It was clear she didn't want me to accompany her this time, so we said goodbye and got into separate cabs. I was relieved. I needed time to process what I had just seen and think about how to shape my observations into a compelling narrative.

Chapter 24

RUSS BEGAN SHOPPING my revised book proposal around in early 2012. But no publishers seemed interested. That winter, Russ called to tell me he was stepping back from full-time work as an agent because of a medical ailment and I was one of the clients he was going to let go. I was devastated. I had put so much work into this project and it didn't look like I would ever get a book contract.

Russ tried to be reassuring.

"Trade publishers are afraid of this kind of project—it's too risky for them," Russ said. "What I would suggest you do is try to sell this book directly to an academic publisher. Ironically, they are more willing to take risks in this day and age. They don't need to make a lot of money."

Knowing how difficult it would be to find another agent, I took his advice. Shula Reinharz, who was then the director of the women's studies program at Brandeis University, suggested I show my book proposal to a friend of hers, Phyllis Deutsch. As it happened, Deutsch was the editor of an academic press, the University Press of New England (UPNE), a consortium of four universities: Brandeis, Northeastern, University of New Hampshire, and Dartmouth College, where Deutsch was also a history professor. Deutsch liked my proposal but said it would need to be revamped to interest an academic press. I needed to do more research, she said, include more studies about sex work here and abroad and make it clear why and how I favored decriminalizing sex work in the United States.

In the midst of revising my proposal yet again, my husband and I moved from Massachusetts to West Virginia. I had been on the lookout for a more stable teaching position. As a women's college, Mount Holyoke College was experiencing financial difficulties mainly because it was having trouble recruiting full-paying female students, many of whom preferred attending co-ed institutions. It became clear that one of the casualties of the college's retrenchment would be its professional writing program. While my three-year contract with Mount Holyoke had been renewed for another two years, I had been informed by college officials that they probably wouldn't be able to renew it a third time. Since our two sons had flown the coop—David had just graduated from college and was doing a year teaching English in Spain and Jake was still in college—I felt free to look for jobs farther afield.

I applied to several tenure-track teaching openings and became a finalist for two positions, one in New Jersey and one at West Virginia University in Morgantown. I was already familiar with Morgantown because my brother had lived in West Virginia for many years, and I had visited him and his family there on occasion. Indeed, my nephew had been Bar Mitzvahed in Morgantown's Tree of Life synagogue in 2006 and my entire family had stayed at the Waterfront Hotel in Morgantown and toured WVU's downtown campus.

I interviewed at both universities and felt much more comfortable with the faculty at WVU. Several of them took me out to dinner at an upscale restaurant and they seemed very welcoming. Even more importantly, they seemed to really care about grooming the next generation of journalists and were excited to have me join them.

By contrast, I was not at all impressed by the physical environs or faculty I met at the New Jersey state university I visited that winter. The university looked like a run-down high school, with lockers lining the halls and overcrowded classrooms, and the journalism faculty was so disorganized they forgot to pick me up at my hotel for the interview. I ended up driving to the campus myself.

In March 2012, I accepted a tenure-track teaching position at West Virginia University and we moved to Morgantown that July. During a whirlwind trip over Memorial Day weekend that year, we had put money down on a stately, three-story Victorian in South Park, the historic district of Morgantown. I was struck by the difference in the standard of living between Massachusetts and West Virginia We had made a decent profit selling our house in Newton after living there for twenty-one years, and we were able to buy a much bigger, more updated house in Morgantown with lovely views for less than half of what we sold the Newton house for. By the time the school year started, my husband had found a social work job and we were ensconced in our new home in South Park.

In between teaching two classes and getting up to speed on how things were done at WVU, I finished revising my proposal for a book that was heavier on research and might appeal to academic presses. I shared the proposal with Phyllis Deutsch again that winter, but she continued to play hard to get. She suggested I do still more research for the book, interviewing experts in countries that had legalized prostitution and reorganizing the manuscript by thematic chapters. I wanted to scream, "You're killing me!" but I couldn't afford to alienate the one editor who had expressed interest in my project. So I grumbled privately to my husband and back to the trenches I went.

Now that we lived only five hours from Bryn Gweled, I saw my parents more often and I was troubled by my mother's growing irritability and failing memory. She seemed increasingly paranoid and for the first time that I could recall lashed out in anger at immigrants whom she said were taking jobs away from native-born Americans. I was baffled. This was the same woman who had let Brazilian soccer players stay at our house for several summers running. But now she railed at Hispanic immigrants whom she was convinced were a blight on the U.S. economy. I tried to talk her into seeing a neurologist but she refused to acknowledge she had a problem. Finally, in November, I got a call from her ear doctor. Mom had failed a hearing test, but she refused to consider a hearing aid and had been quite belligerent with the doctor.

"I think she has a problem that goes beyond her hearing," the ear doctor said. "I can get her in with a neurologist friend of mine pretty quickly. He'll see her on my say so."

In December 2012, as soon as my classes that semester were over, I drove to my parents' home in Bryn Gweled. The next day we went to see Dr. Rosenfeld, who, as I had discovered, was a highly respected neurologist. He questioned Mom and gave her some cognitive tests. That same afternoon, sitting behind a big desk in his office, Rosenfeld told Mom that she was in the beginning stages of Alzheimer's. She should consider taking some medication that might forestall further mental deterioration, he said. Mom sat there with a stone-cold look on her face and said nothing. Finally, I thanked the doctor and said we needed to talk things over as family and would be in touch.

Mom flew into a rage as soon as we left the doctor's office.

"I don't have Alzheimer's," she cried. "No one in my family has had it. Look at Aunt Ida!" She was referring to her mother's sister, who had lived into her nineties and was lucid until the day she died.

"This is all your father's fault," Mom said. "I hurt my head when I tripped over his briefcase, and I haven't been right since." This was not the first time I had heard about Mom hitting her head when she accompanied Dad to a doctor's appointment. We had been over this ground before.

"Hitting your head may have exacerbated things," I said, trying to be as patient as I could. "But you were having memory problems even before you tripped over Dad's briefcase."

"I don't have Alzheimer's, Ali," Mom said. "Leave me alone!"

The next day, I drove back to Morgantown. Mom was still in denial and nothing had been resolved.

That spring, one of my sources mentioned that Desiree Alliance, an organization run for and by sex workers, would be holding its bi-annual conference in Las Vegas, Nevada over the summer. I talked to one of the organizers of the conference and after running it by her board, she said I could attend as long as I didn't use anyone's names without getting permission first. She also gave me the names of several insiders connected with the sex trade in Nevada and suggested I talk to them. In a series of phone interviews, I learned that Nevada was the sole state in the nation where prostitution remained legal but only in rural counties with less than 400,000 people.

I was astonished to discover that despite Las Vegas's moniker as Sin City, sex work was not legal there or in any of the state's large urban areas. According to my sources, however, casinos in Las Vegas and Reno looked the other way when well-dressed escorts picked up men at their bars. I decided to try to visit one or two of the legal brothels in Nevada while I was there for the Desiree Alliance conference. A source gave me the name and contact information for Jeremy Lazur, the press liaison for

Sheri's Ranch, an upscale brothel about forty-five minutes east of Las Vegas. Since Nevada's brothels were often hounded by hostile media who had heard horror stories from anti-prostitution crusaders, I think Lazur had a hard time believing I was who I said I was—an author who had done extensive research on the sex industry and believed that adult sex work should be legalized or at the very least decriminalized. After an exchange of emails and a lengthy phone conversation, Lazur said he would clear my visit to Sheri's Ranch when I came to Nevada in July.

At the end of June, I flew up to Martha's Vineyard, where my parents spent most of every summer. Mom always made at least one trip back to Bryn Gweled during the summer to check up on their house, mow the lawn, and pay bills. At one point, she confided there was another reason: "I need a break from your father," she said. "I can only take so much of him."

To get home, she would take a bus from Woods Hole to Providence, hop on another bus that took her to the Port Authority in New York City and then walk seven blocks to New York's Penn Station, where she would catch a train to Trenton. There, a friend from Bryn Gweled would pick her up and drive her home. But that summer, I noticed that Mom's memory problems and irritability were worse than ever. I was concerned that she might get lost traveling home on her own, particularly since she always walked by herself from the Port Authority bus station to the train station, dragging a suitcase. When I voiced my concerns, she exploded.

"You're ruining my life Ali," she yelled. "I'm going!"

Dad tried to talk her out of the trip back to BG too, but she was adamant. She was going home come hell or high water. Finally, Dad agreed that he would go with her, even though he didn't really want to leave the Vineyard. He loved puttering around the house, painting and making repairs wherever necessary. And when he wasn't fixing up the house, he enjoyed sailing his sixteen-foot Bullseye and swimming in Nantucket Sound. But he wasn't about to let his wife travel home by herself. Even so, I was worried about them. Dad, at the age of ninety, was afraid of falling and he walked much slower than Mom did. I was afraid she would leave him in the dust on their way to Penn Station.

Before they left, I made a trip of my own—to Las Vegas. The Desiree Alliance conference was held at the Alexis Park Hotel, a resort-style lodging with three pools a few blocks from the strip. Even though sex work was officially illegal in Las Vegas, I soon learned that the law was arbitrarily enforced. Yellow page advertisements for escorts could be found in every hotel room in the city, and hawkers handed out escorts' cards on the city's famously gaudy strip. The Las Vegas police department only used its powers of arrest to corral streetwalkers who were minorities or obviously drunk. Indeed, one of the organizers of the Desiree Alliance conference was picked up with an African American friend, also a sex worker, simply because they appeared tipsy and jaywalked across a street. They were held in a jail cell overnight before being released.

At the conference, I met and interviewed many sex workers, both women and men, ranging from streetwalkers to high-end escorts. I heard several stirring keynote speeches and attended a number of workshops, including one late afternoon panel titled "Hooker-nomics: The Business of Sex or Your Pleasure is my Business." I got there early enough to snag a seat, but all the other seats were soon taken, and an overflow crowd of men and women sat in the aisle or stood against the back wall. Everyone was dressed for the heat (the air-conditioning in the conference rooms wasn't working too well), some in shorts and sleeveless T-shirts, others in cool flowing skirts and low-cut blouses. There were three female sex workers on the panel, along with a woman who ran an erotic website and a male escort who went by the name of Legendary Dave.

Dave explained that he required a 50 percent deposit on all his appointments because that weeded out people who were not serious about meeting with him. Dave said he only accepted cash deposits and asked clients to FedEx them to him.

"I try to stay away from credit cards and PayPal," he said. "PayPal froze my account and kept a couple of thousand dollars for a year. So I don't use PayPal anymore."

Dave, who had strolled into the room barefoot and bare-chested, said he only met clients at a separate apartment near his house. "I'm a parent and I wasn't comfortable doing in calls, having people in my home."

As Dave and the other panelists explained how they conducted their businesses, I saw people around the room scribble furiously in notepads or tablets. Someone walking by might think they had stumbled upon a typical corporate conference, and in one very real sense, they would be right. The women and men in this room were serious about their work and intent of building successful careers. So what if those careers were not exactly legit.

A few days later, I drove out to Sheri's Ranch, located in the dusty desert town of Pahrump about forty-five minutes east of Las Vegas. I had rented a car for the day and made sure I had a full tank of gas since I had no idea where I was going. As I drove down the highway into an increasingly remote and mountainous desert terrain, I wondered just what I was getting myself into.

Sheri's Ranch looked like a big sprawling resort set in the middle of nowhere. A bouncer asked my name before letting me in the imposing mahogany doors and instructed me to wait in the brothel's airy lounge until Jeremy Lazur could collect me. I was impressed. Plush, floral-patterned sofas were arranged in the center of the room, attractive impressionist paintings adorned the walls and a grand piano sat in one corner. Light poured in from elegant French doors and windows at the back of the lounge.

Lazur introduced me to Chuck Lee, a Las Vegas businessman who had co-owned Sheri's Ranch since 2001. He was a large man in his sixties dressed in an expensively tailored suit. Lee and I sat down on one of the sofas in the lounge.

"What draws customers here is that they know they're not going to bring something home with them," Lee told me. He explained that mandatory condom use was a non-negotiable rule and no drugs were allowed inside—workers' suitcases were searched each time they came to work. Lee then told me a little bit about himself. He was a former homicide detective and had been the chief investigator for the district attorney in Clark County (which includes Las Vegas and its exurbs.) Lee owned several successful car dealerships before he bought into

Sheri's Ranch. I later learned from talking with a researcher at the University of Nevada that most of the legal brothels in Nevada were owned by businessmen like Lee, with close ties to the state's political infrastructure.

A little while later, I was introduced to "Anna," a young woman with radiantly clear skin, luminous dark green eyes, and a sweet smile. Anna, who had been assigned to give me a tour, wore a short low-cut cocktail dress that hugged her butt and showed off her figure. Yet she was not what anyone would consider exotic. Indeed, she reminded me of the girl next door. Anna grew up in a middle-class home in a suburb of Philadelphia. Although her parents both worked, they had a large family and weren't able to help Anna with her college tuition. As a result, she had racked up considerable student debt, which she was trying to pay off by working at Sheri's Ranch.

"I wish I'd known about this place sooner, I could have made more money," Anna said. In the four years she had worked at Sheri's Ranch beginning when she was twenty-seven, she had not only retired her student debt but was now helping her husband through graduate school. Her husband, she said, was supportive of her job. "He actually finds it exciting. It turns him on a bit."

The first stop on our tour was a room Anna called the formal dining room. "This is where a gentleman can take you out to dinner and clothing is optional," she said. In the center of the room was a small, oval table draped with an elegant tablecloth and set for two. Anna smiled sweetly. "If he wants a blow job under the table, there is a kneeling pillow and a splatter platter. Although now that everyone has to wear condoms, there's no splatter."

I laughed and wondered how many times Anna had used that punchline.

Shortly after I arrived at Sheri's Ranch, a young couple walked in, the woman hanging nervously on her partner's arm. They were from Iceland, I later found out, and wanted to see a line-up before deciding which sex worker to choose for their threesome. The line-up was an old tradition in Nevada brothels. When customers arrived, all workers who weren't occupied with customers had to come to the main lounge and present themselves. I was not allowed to view the line-up that afternoon because of privacy concerns, but someone explained the drill to me afterward.

During the line-up, each sex worker would step forward and introduce herself. They were only permitted to say "Hi" and give their names before returning to the line. And then the customers chose which women they wanted to party with. Groups of men could also arrange private parties with several sex workers. According to a menu of services written on a large poster in the main lounge, such parties started at $1,000 and went on up. Through the sun-lit windows lining the back of the lounge, I could see a pool and several bungalows in the backyard.

"That's where the private parties are held," Anna said. "Each bungalow has a different theme. There's the King Arthur room (replete with a statue of a knight in armor], the safari room, where you can take a walk on the wild side." She said all this with straight face. "We also have a Roman room, a room with the theme of Arabian nights, and a sixties room."

I must have looked bewildered, because Anna added, "You know, it comes with shag rug, lava lamp. We call it our Austin Powers room." I laughed, thinking that whoever came up with such outlandish names must have been high.

We strolled down a long hallway into what she said was the favorite room on the tour: the dungeon. It had black padded walls, on which chains and an assortment of other painful-looking equipment were mounted. In one corner of the room stood a large black leather chair Anna referred to as the "forced orgasm chair," where customers could be tied and dominated. A large black leather couch sat in the center of the room in front of a small stage with a shiny pole for dancing.

"Customers have to sign our waiver that we're not responsible if someone gets hurt," Anna said. I must have looked a bit concerned because she quickly added, "You can also book this room for bachelor parties."

Before the tour ended, Anna gave me her email address so I could contact her if I had any follow-up questions. Earlier, Jeremy Lazur had said I could talk to another brothel worker, a twentysomething whose working name was Tatiana. She had worked at the brothel for several years to pay for her schooling while she was in college. Tatiana now worked as a biologist but still came to the brothel on occasion to supplement her income, Lazur said. A blonde beauty with dark come-hither eyes, Tatiana was the woman who had been picked out of the line-up earlier that afternoon by the Icelandic couple. Lazur said she was still occupied and wouldn't be able to talk to me after all. I asked if I could continue talking with Anna but he said that "things were picking up" and she was needed elsewhere. Although he was polite, it was clear he wanted my visit to end. I didn't quite understand why; perhaps Chuck Lee hadn't liked some of the questions I asked, or perhaps Lazur was just getting nervous about the amount of time I was spending at the ranch. I didn't know but I knew enough not to press things. I thanked Anna for the tour, shook her hand, and took my leave. As I drove away, I couldn't help wondering what it would be like to come back to Sheri's Ranch with my husband for a threesome.

A week after I returned to the Vineyard, my parents left for Bryn Gweled so Mom could mow the lawn and collect the mail. I welcomed the quiet time to myself so I could work on my book, but even so I was worried. I knew Dad wouldn't be able to walk the seven blocks between Port Authority and Penn Station and I hoped Mom would not give him a hard time about taking a taxi. I called home that evening, anxious to hear about their trip. Mom answered the phone on the fourth ring. Yes, their trip went fine. But she seemed harried and reluctant, as usual, to stay on the phone. "I have a lot to do, Ali," she said. "We'll see you in a few days."

Chapter 25

IN THE QUIET that followed, I wrote a second chapter about my visit to Sheri's Ranch and shipped the new proposal to Phyllis Deutsch. Mom and Dad returned to the island without incident and later that week, I drove back to West Virginia. In early August, a week before classes were scheduled to resume, I attended a journalism conference in Washington, D.C., where I bumped into Toni Locy, a former colleague of mine from the *Boston Globe*. Toni had just published a book about how to cover the courts and she introduced me to her editor, who worked for an academic press and was at the conference networking with potential authors. The editor expressed an interest in seeing my book proposal, so I sent it to her. A few weeks later, she replied that she was interested in making me an offer. I emailed Phyllis Deutsch to let her know I had another offer on the table. At that point, Deutsch said UPNE would also make me an offer for the book. I couldn't believe my luck; leverage really did work after all.

The UPNE offer was better; it gave me better royalties and a small advance, which the other academic press didn't provide. I didn't hold it against Phyllis that she had taken so long to make up her mind; in the end, she had pushed me to put together a better, more comprehensive proposal. I signed a book contract with UPNE in the fall of 2013 and felt consumed by relief. Obtaining a book contract meant that I was on course to get tenure at WVU but more importantly, it meant that all the work I'd done over the past four years would not be in vain.

That Thanksgiving, my parents arrived at our house in Morgantown, bearing three packed suitcases. After my husband had taken the suitcases up to the guest room, Mom motioned for me to come up with her. She shut the door and started unpacking two of the suitcases. Inside she had crammed all kinds of clothes (not just for cold weather) as well as two heavy objects wrapped in tissue paper. She pulled them out to show me. They were ornate tiles with blue-green swirling patterns on them.

"These Turkish tiles are very valuable," she whispered. "I'm giving you both of them too." And then she added, "I'm not going back to BG. Can I stay with you?"

I was stunned. The previous spring, my parents had finally agreed to put their names on a waiting list for an assisted living center in Morgantown, where they would be close to me and my brother, who lived thirty minutes away in Clarksburg. Mom was more than ready to move. She badly wanted to leave Bryn Gweled, her home for sixty-five years. She wouldn't say why but I knew the reason. She was embarrassed by her deteriorating mental state and did not want her friends and neighbors to see her this way. But Dad didn't want to leave; he had made it clear he wanted to die in Bryn Gweled. He only agreed to go on the center's waiting list after my brothers intervened and talked him into it. We all knew that Mom needed more assistance than she was getting at home. But when my parents finally put their names on the waiting list for the Village at Heritage Point and paid a deposit, we were told it might take up to a year to get them an apartment on the independent living side of the center.

Now, here it was six months later, and Mom had reached her breaking point. "I can't stay with your father," she said. "He's not good for me. This all started when I tripped over his damn briefcase. I've got to get away from him."

I tried to convince her that she needed to go home with her husband of sixty-six years, that it was only a matter of time before we would get them into the Village. But she was having none of it. Finally, I tried a different tack.

"Dad needs you with him," I said. "He's getting very frail." Indeed, Dad had already fallen once while visiting us; his legs just went out from under him on a walk. "What happens if something happens to him and he's all alone? He needs you."

Mom flung up an arm. "Okay, but can you look around for a place we can stay in Morgantown until the Village has an opening?" And then she again pushed the heavy tiles toward me. "I want you to have these."

I sighed. "Mom, it wouldn't be fair for me to take both of them. Remember, we agreed that Linda gets one of them."

This wasn't the first time Mom had acted irrationally. She used to have an extensive collection of valuable Chinese vases and bowls that she had bought over the years. By 2013, she had sold most of them, and during a previous visit to Morgantown, she brought the remaining pottery to my house.

"They're yours," she said.

I knew she didn't really mean that, that the generous and scrupulously fair mother I had grown up with would never behave like that. But as is typical of some Alzheimer's patients, Mom had become paranoid and angry at the world. I told her I would divide up the bowls equally between Linda, Paul, and I (Stuart had already said he didn't want any) and that would be that.

Now she was trying to pull the same stunt with the two tiles.

"I'm not taking them back with me," she said firmly. "That's all there is to it."

I told her I would keep both of them here and then bring one up to the Vineyard and give it to Linda when she visited my parents, as she usually did over the summer. Mom agreed and a few days later, she reluctantly returned to Bryn Gweled with my dad.

In mid-February, Mom called me on the phone. "I'm dying," she announced with great fanfare.

I was baffled; what did she mean? She had complained on occasion that her stomach hurt, but my brother, an oncologist, said the pain she was experiencing probably came from scar tissue left over from surgery she had had the previous year for diverticulitis. I had repeatedly pressed her to go see an internist close to Bryn Gweled, but she said she didn't have one that she liked or trusted. She had apparently fired her most recent primary care doctor for reasons I didn't fully understand. I realized we had to get Mom to Morgantown, where I could be more actively involved in her care. I mentioned to Jan, a friend of ours who happened to work at The Village, that we were going to check out another assisted living center in Bridgeport, near where my brother lived. It was taking too long to get my parents into the Village.

A week later, we got a call from the Village. A long-time tenant had just died and an apartment had opened up on the independent living side. Jan had apparently told the Village's director of sales and marketing that we were looking elsewhere and she had moved my parents to the top of the list. It took the center a month to rehab the apartment, replace the appliances and the carpeting and repaint the walls. We moved our parents into a lovely two-bedroom apartment in the Village the first week of April.

Now that my parents were living ten minutes from me, I could see how quickly Mom was deteriorating. A year before, she had described her mental state to me. "It's like there's a fog in my mind," she said. That summer, she repeatedly asked me to procure drugs so she could put herself out of her misery.

"I don't want to live like this, Ali," she said.

When I told her that I couldn't procure a lethal cocktail for her—it was illegal—she retorted, "If you don't get me those drugs, I'm going to walk out into Nantucket Sound and drown myself." After hearing that, I told Dad to make sure she never went to the beach by herself.

It had been months since Mom had threatened to kill herself, but she was no longer the vibrant, outgoing woman she once had been. She didn't want to socialize with any of her new neighbors at the Village; she didn't even want to go down to the dining area for lunch or dinner (except when Paul or I were visiting). Dad had taken to ordering their dinners and he would go down and pick them up so they could eat in the apartment. Dad had always made his own breakfast and now he began making lunch for the two of them as well. Mom had stopped cooking months ago, since she could no longer remember how to cook and Dad was afraid she might leave the stove on. Whenever she came over to my house in South Park for dinner (and we invited them over at least once a week), she would sit next to me on the loveseat in our den and complain bitterly about Dad and how she wasn't safe with him.

One of the first things I did when the Village told me a spot had opened up was to arrange doctors' appointments for Mom and Dad at WVU Medicine in Morgantown. But I couldn't get Mom in to see her designated internist until mid-May. When I took her to the appointment and the doctor, a young woman who was wearing a head scarf, asked her if she was experiencing any pain, she acknowledged that her stomach hurt. But she didn't want to talk about it.

"How much pain are you having on a scale of one to ten?" the doctor asked.

Mom looked down at the floor and whispered, "Four."

The doctor gave her a physical exam and found nothing. "I could prescribe something that might ease your stomach." She didn't mention doing any tests.

"No," Mom said. "I don't take drugs."

Not taking medication had always been a point of pride for her. While my dad was on at least ten different prescriptions—for his heart, his kidneys, his elevated PSAs, you name it—Mom wouldn't even take aspirin for a headache. And she wasn't about to start now. I regret that I didn't push Mom harder to have tests done to find out what was bothering her, but it was clear she just wanted to get out of the doctor's office and go home.

The same thing happened when we finally got in to see a gerontologist in early June. He too asked her about her pain level was and she again said four. She mentioned that her stomach hurt but all the gerontologist wanted to talk about was getting her back on medication for Alzheimer's. Mom had been wearing an Exelon patch (a medication for Alzheimer's), but a month before, she had decided she didn't want to take it any longer and no amount of talking—by the doctor, me or my oncologist brother—could convince her otherwise.

In mid-June, my parents drove up to the Vineyard for the summer. When I visited over July 4th, I could see that Mom had deteriorated even further. She was no longer joining us for our daily walks to Edgartown Harbor after dinner, and she wasn't walking anywhere by herself. She didn't want to go to the beach, she didn't want to do anything. I offered to bring her back with me, but she didn't want to leave the Vineyard. My sister, Linda, was coming in two weeks and she wanted to see her. I didn't push her; I was racing to finish a draft of my book and would be traveling for much of the month.

In mid-July, I drove to Washington, D.C. to do some pre-arranged interviews for my book. First, I visited an outreach center for streetwalkers known as Helping Individual Prostitutes Survive (HIPS) in northeast Washington. I had interviewed the executive director of the center a few weeks earlier and she had arranged for me to meet with several transgender streetwalkers who used the center's services. I also had arranged to meet with the director of FAIR Girls, a nonprofit organization that helped girls who have been trafficked into the sex trade. While both administrators opposed laws that allow police to arrest sex workers, they came at the issue from very different points of view. Cyndee Clay, the head of HIPS, supported wholesale decriminalization because she believed arresting adult sex workers and their clients was a massive waste of resources that could be better used to help these women get to the point where sex work was a choice instead of an economic necessity. Andrea Powell, the director of FAIR Girls, on the other hand, supported laws that would criminalize the clients, regardless of whether they were buying sex from adults or underage youths. I felt it was important to have both perspectives in my book.

In late July, I got a call from Linda. This was the first time she had seen Mom since last year.

"There's something very wrong with Mom," she said. "I've never seen her this bad."

"I know," I said. "It's as if she's given up the will to live." I suggested that we arrange to have Mom or both my parents join Linda when she left the island and took the bus from Woods Hole to Logan airport. I said I would buy them nonstop tickets to Pittsburgh and pick them up there. But Mom wouldn't listen to Linda or me.

"I'm not flying," she said flatly.

A year earlier, my brother, Stuart, had arranged a bucket list trip for both our immediate families—a week-long rafting trip that wove down the Colorado River through the Grand Canyon. If I had known how sick Mom was, I don't think I would have gone on that trip. But at this point, I didn't realize the extent of Mom's illness and so I went. In early August, my husband, our two grown sons, and I met my brother, his girlfriend and his two sons, who were about the same age as mine and good buddies, in Las Vegas. The next day, we took a shuttle bus to the upper reaches of the Colorado River and hopped on the large rubber rafts that would take us through the Grand Canyon. There was no cell phone coverage on the river so I couldn't check to see how Mom was doing. Nor could I access my emails or the internet to do any reporting for my book. It was refreshing to be out of touch with the world, and we had a truly amazing trip, full of gorgeous vistas and exciting plunges through dangerous rapids. We hiked almost daily into the wilderness along the river and saw thrilling waterfalls, ancient rock formations, and breathtakingly beautiful turquoise pools. We camped out every night on sandy spits by the river, where the crew made delicious meals for the forty-odd people on the trip and we slept on cots under the stars every night. (The cots had metal legs that scorpions apparently couldn't climb.) We had brought our own wine and beer and at my request, my husband had even brought along a solar shower, a plastic contraption filled with water that warmed up in the sun during the day and when hooked to a tree, turned into a functional shower. I was the only one on the trip who showered that week, although I had to bathe in a bikini since there wasn't any privacy at the campsites. Only one person went overboard during our trip, a guide who forgot to hold on during our plunge into one of the rapids. Fortunately, he knew how to ride the washing machine and emerged at the bottom of the rapids unscathed.

When we got back to Morgantown, I called my parents and was relieved to hear that Mom sounded like herself, happy that we'd had a good time and were safely back home. They drove back to Morgantown themselves the following Friday and the minute I saw Mom, I knew something was very wrong. She could barely walk a few steps before saying she was tired and needed to sit down. Her legs were badly swollen. She told me she and Dad had gone to the hospital on Martha's Vineyard while we were away to find out what was going on and the ER doctors had done a bunch of tests. But my parents left before getting the test results because, Mom said, "Dad was hungry and wanted to go home for dinner."

The following Monday, I called Martha's Vineyard Hospital and asked them to please fax their test results to Mom's internist in

Morgantown, the same doctor whom she had seen in May. They did the next day, but the doctor didn't read the results until that Thursday (after I had called three times and screamed at her nurse.) As soon as the doctor saw the results, she ordered an emergency CAT scan for Mom the following day.

The next day, I drove Mom to the hospital, which had valet parking, and helped maneuver her in a wheelchair and up to the imaging unit. As we sat in the waiting room and Mom sipped the dye concoction she was supposed to drink before the CAT scan, she was tired but very much her usual self.

"I'm grateful that you're here with me, Ali," she said. "You know, I'm not afraid to die."

I squeezed Mom's hand. "I know. I'm glad I'm here too. Let's see what the CAT scan shows."

Shortly before six that evening, I was just finishing dinner at home when my cell rang. It was Mom's doctor. "Your mom has advanced pancreatic cancer. I'm very sorry."

I gasped. "Shit," was all I could say.

The doctor cleared her throat. "I'm not sure it would help at this point but we could start aggressive treatment right away. Do you know if she wants that?"

I took a deep breath. "I doubt it, but let me call my brother and we'll get back to you. Thanks for letting me know."

I hung up the phone and started crying. My husband, who was a social worker for the Morgantown hospice, came over and put his arm around me. "I'm so sorry, but look at this way: this is her ticket out. We can put her on hospice and make sure she's comfortable to the end."

I wiped my tears away with a sleeve. "Let me call Paul. We should tell her tonight."

When I told Paul, he said he would drive up to Morgantown immediately and together we would give Mom the news. As an oncologist, Paul often had to relay bad news to patients, and I knew he'd be better at it than me. I was a basket case.

An hour later, we were sitting in the living room of my parents' apartment at the Village. Mom was seated in her favorite wing chair and I sat on the couch next to her. Paul squatted in front of her and said, "The CAT scan results came back. You have advanced pancreatic cancer."

Mom sat back in her chair and her lips curved into a small smile. At that moment, it came to me: she had known all along she was terminally ill but had not wanted to call any attention to herself for fear we would try to coerce her into treatment.

Through a fog, I heard Paul ask, "Do you want to try to treat this?"

"No," Mom said. "I'm ready to go."

The next day, Mom entered hospice in her own apartment. By Monday, they had set up a hospital bed in the living room so she could sleep comfortably, and a hospice nurse came to check on her every other day. One afternoon, while Mom was sitting up in her hospital bed, she looked over at me and the hospice nurse and said, "I'm going to see my family."

Huh, I thought. Her family, or least Dad and I, were right there. What did she mean? The hospice nurse said quietly, "She's talking about all of her family who have died. She knows she's going to meet them on the other side. We hear that a lot of from our terminally ill patients."

All I could do was nod in amazement.

Before we found out about Mom's diagnosis, I had been planning to fly to Boston the following Wednesday so I could interview the head of the vice squad for the Providence, Rhode Island, police department for my sex work book. I had emailed him with some questions about a chapter I was writing about a long-time loophole in Rhode Island's law that essentially decriminalized indoor sex work for two decades. He had been very responsive and offered to show me around should I have a chance to visit Providence and its famous sex clubs and spas. So I decided to take him up on the offer. I was then going to take a ferry to Martha's Vineyard so I could say goodbye to my son Jake who was leaving with his long-time girlfriend to spend nine months in Spain, teaching English as my older son had done a few years prior. My husband was planning to drive up Friday and we were going to help Jake and his girlfriend close the Vineyard house down and then drive back on Monday, Labor Day. But now that my mom was in hospice,

I didn't think I should go. I didn't want to be away from her for any length of time.

I had talked to Mom before about the book I was working on, but the few times I mentioned plans to meet a sex worker or visit a brothel, she had always expressed concern.

"Are you sure that's safe, Ali?" she would invariably ask. So I had stopped giving her the gritty details about my book project. When I discussed my quandary about my upcoming trip to her, I didn't mention that I would be shadowing a police officer in Providence, just that I was planning to spend a few days on the Vineyard saying goodbye to my son and his girlfriend.

"You should go, Ali," Mom said. "Jake and Dina need help closing the house down and I know you want to say goodbye to them. Don't worry about me; I'm not very good company now anyway."

This was the Mom I knew, always thinking of others rather than herself. Late Wednesday afternoon, after visiting her for a few hours, I told her that I loved her and gave her a big hug.

"I'll be back soon," I said and walked of the room, tears blurring my sight.

Chapter 26

MY FLIGHT TO Boston that evening was delayed, and I didn't get in until 11:30 pm. I stayed overnight with a friend of mine who waited up till midnight for me. The next morning, I took the bus down to Providence. I was picked up at the bus terminal by Anthony Sauro, the head of the vice squad. Sauro, a fit fifty-seven-year-old cop with a shock of white hair, drove me around to two of the Asian massage parlors in town.

"These are full-service," he said, meaning clients could get hand jobs and oral sex in addition to massages. "The girls are all Asian. They're coming up from New York."

Sauro told me he thought adult consensual prostitution should be decriminalized. "It's just like marijuana. If we decriminalized it, we could focus on trafficking. We get a lot of people asking what we're doing about trafficking. A lot of pressure is coming down on us."

That very afternoon, Sauro said, his squad was planning to raid a brothel in the West End, a poor, largely minority neighborhood of Providence. The brothel mainly serviced Guatemalan immigrants who worked in the city's restaurants, he said. Was I interested in coming along for the ride? I most certainly was. I had interviewed a number of law enforcement officials for my book but this would be the first time I would actually get to see the police in action.

Shortly after 1:30 pm, Sauro, with me in the passenger seat, parked his unmarked Passat in a small private parking lot on Waverly Street a few houses down from the alleged brothel. A few yards in either direction sat two large unmarked SUVs, one white, one black with tinted glass. Inside were four men from Saura's vice squad and two women from the U.S. Department of Homeland Security. The women were part of the stakeout because the federal government sometimes prosecuted cases of trafficking across state lines. I heard the voice of Leo Pichs, one of the undercover cops and the only Spanish-speaking member of the squad, crackle over the walkie talkie.

"We're going to wait till we get a couple of bodies in there, and then we just fucking whack it," Pichs said.

Ten minutes into the stakeout, Pichs's voice again came over the walkie talkie. "Two guys going in. Looks good. We'll give it a few minutes."

Five more minutes passed, although it seemed like an eternity, and finally, Sauro said into his walkie talkie, "Okay, Leo's, let go." He wheeled out of the parking lot in time for me to see the two SUVs pull up in front of the brothel. The four men and two women jumped and ran down the driveway into the back of the building, their handguns drawn. Sauro pulled into the driveway after them.

"I'd be rushing in with them, but I don't want to leave you," he said. A few minutes later, he got a hand signal—it was safe for us to go in.

Inside, two men sat handcuffed in the small spare living room, a stocky Guatemalan immigrant (who turned out to be the unlucky john) and a skinny older man wearing a BOSS T-Shirt and a golfing cap. Sauro said he was the pimp who ran the brothel. Two women (who were not handcuffed) sat on chairs in different rooms, one in a bedroom, the other in what must have once been a dining room. The walls of the first-floor apartment were dirty and bare; rough gray mats were duct-taped to the hardwood floor, and there was a dead cockroach in the kitchen. A soda bottle lay on its side on a small table, spilling Mountain Dew over a box of Newport cigarettes, in front of a TV that was still tuned to the Spanish channel.

If this was a brothel, it was a big step down from the bordellos that Julie Moya ran in New York and a world away from the lavish ambiance at Sheri's Ranch in Nevada. And yet the woman who sat on a chair near the spilled bottle, a towel wrapped around her bikini underwear, was pretty and slim with streaked blonde hair, immaculate French nails, and big green eyes, carefully made up. She told me that her name was Juanita Delacruz; she was twenty-eight and came from the Dominican Republic. She said she was an exotic dancer in New York City and had come up to Providence on her own volition, to earn money to pay her rent.

The other woman, stocky and dark-haired, wearing capri pants and a low-cut tank top, sat in the bedroom next to a tousled queen-size bed that took up most of the room. She sat slumped over, her head in her hands. She looked up when I came in and in response to my questions, said she was from Mexico. In halting English, she explained that she had been cleaning houses in New York City but had chosen to come to Providence to earn more money to send back to her family in Mexico.

After I finished speaking with the women, Sauro took me aside and said he didn't plan to arrest them. "We treat them as victims." But he added they would probably be taken down to the police station so that detectives could interrogate them about the men who operated the brothel.

Pichs appeared in the living room, holding a sack. "We've got the money, the ledgers, photographs, we just have to get the girls downtown." The two handcuffed men were ushered out by two uniformed policemen who had been summoned after the raid, and the two women from Homeland Security took the women away.

A week later, Sauro told me that the Dominican sex worker, who was in the country legally, was not arrested. But the Mexican woman turned out to be an illegal immigrant and she was deported, even though Sauro acknowledged that neither of the women had been trafficked.

After the raid, Sauro drove me back to the bus terminal. Along the way, I asked him if he thought that raids like this one were a worthwhile use of police resources.

"It's a quality of life issue," he said. "[The brothel] is in a neighborhood where kids are riding bikes. There could have been trafficking victims involved."

Only there weren't. As I discovered from talking with law enforcement experts, very few Mexican immigrants were trafficked into the sex trade. Most of them, like the woman who was detained that day in Providence, were selling sex by choice.

That afternoon, I took the bus to New Bedford and just made the Seastreak ferry to Martha's Vineyard. On the hour-long ride, I watched as the sun began its descent in the west. It was a heartbreakingly beautiful sight. Jake and Dina met me at the ferry and we had dinner at a popular Italian restaurant in Oak Bluffs. I was exhausted but happy to be on the island with my son and his girlfriend.

The next day, I called my parents and my sister-in-law, Paul's wife, answered the phone.

"Your mom is asking for you," Laurie said. "Here she is."

I heard my mom's voice come on the phone. "Hi honey, where are you?" Her voice sounded faint. She had obviously forgotten where I was. I tried to sounds chipper.

"Remember, Mom, I'm on the Vineyard, saying goodbye to Jake and Dina and helping them close the house for the season," I said. "But I'll be back real soon."

There was a faint sigh on the other end of the phone and my mom's voice dropped away. I could sense that she was fading fast. Then and there I decided to fly back early. I booked a flight for Sunday afternoon. Jim said he would help Jake finish closing the house without me.

That Sunday, I took the bus to Boston's Logan airport, but my flight to Pittsburgh was delayed. I finally got into Morgantown around midnight and debated whether I should go directly to my parents' apartment or drive home and try to get some sleep. I decided not to go to the Village because I didn't want to disturb my dad. I went home to an empty house and finally fell asleep sometime after 1 am. Around 6 am, I startled awake, overwhelmed with the certainty that I had to get over to the Village right away.

Shortly before 7 am I walked into my parents' apartment to find Mom still alive but in a restless sleep or light coma. I squeezed her hand and told her I was there. She was obviously in pain, clutching the bedsheets with one hand. When I had called her apartment from the airport yesterday afternoon, my brother, Paul, told me he had started giving her morphine to ease her pain and she was starting to sleep more soundly. I found the morphine, gave her a few drops followed by a sip of ginger ale. But she still seemed uncomfortable, although she never opened her eyes.

"It hurts," she mumbled at one point.

I called the hospice nurse, who was there within twenty minutes. Even though she was a young woman who had just begun working for Morgantown hospice, she knew exactly what do to. She said Mom had soiled herself, so she deftly changed her into a clean dry nightgown and fresh sheets. She also gave her some more morphine. Mom slept through the whole thing. After the nurse left, Mom seemed more comfortable. I sat by her side, holding her hand. I told her that I loved her and that she had been the best Mom any daughter could ever hope for.

My brother, Paul, walked into the apartment around 10 am and Mom died at 10:30 am, with the two of us by her side. My initial emotion was relief—Mom was finally out of her misery. But in the weeks and months to come, I was racked by intense guilt that I wasn't there when she fell into a coma. That I didn't get to say goodbye to the woman I loved most in the world.

Chapter 27

WE HELD MOM'S funeral in the Philadelphia area, which was where my parents wanted to be buried. I remember waking up the morning of the funeral at the hotel and jotting down a few words to say about Mom at the service. I finished my brief remarks by saying:

"My mother made her mark in so many ways but to me the most significant impact she had on me and my brothers and sister was her firm and confident conviction that we were special, that we could do anything we put our minds to and that we would succeed. Whatever I have accomplished in this life so far I owe to my mother's unwavering love for and belief in me."

The chapel at Goldsteins Rosenbergs Funeral Home in Southampton was packed with relatives, friends, and former neighbors of my parents. Several local residents came up after the service to tell us how Mom had helped them when she was a township supervisor. After burying Mom in the same cemetery where her own parents were interned, we drove back to Bryn Gweled for a memorial luncheon, which had been generously arranged by my parents' friends on the homestead. Lots of people came, including good friends of mine from Princeton, New Jersey and New York. A steady loop of pictures featuring Mom ran on a projector screen while guests ate tuna salad, chicken salad, bagels and lox from my mom's favorite deli, Ben and Irv's. I had broken down and cried at the cemetery, but somehow managed to keep it together as guests offered condolences and shared stories about Mom. I was operating on automatic pilot, emotionally numb the entire time.

When we returned to Morgantown, I resumed teaching and working on my book. I had been given a course reduction after getting my book contract so I only had to teach one class that fall. As a result, I was able to finish a draft of my manuscript earlier than expected. I had written fifteen chapters based on specific themes, which included the history of prostitution in the U.S.; the evolution of the modern sex workers movement; why women and men do sex work; the truth about sex trafficking; how bad laws lead to bad law enforcement; Nevada's two-faced approach to sex work; the Rhode Island story; as well as two chapters on sex work in other countries. I tried to weave the stories of the individual sex workers I had interviewed in amid the studies and policy suggestions. Julie Moya's poignant story emerged as a central narrative throughout the book, and Elle St. Claire, Jillian, and the transgender streetwalkers I met in D.C. were also featured in its pages, among other sex workers I had met in the course of researching the book. In early November, I shipped a copy of the manuscript off to Phyllis Deutsch and heaved a big sigh of relief.

With time on my hands, I then turned my attention to a very different labor of love: getting Mom's engrossing account of her own grandmother's life in Czarist Russia published. Her grandmother, whose name was Gittle, had started writing her memoir in a black and white composition notebook when she was in her eighties but died before she could finish it. Her only daughter, Aunt Anna, blind and near death herself, had passed the memoir onto my mom. The only problem was that Gittle had written her story in a hodgepodge of Russian, German, Hebrew, Yiddish, and English. Mom spent a long time looking for someone who could translate it. She finally found an elderly gentleman in Philadelphia who had done some translating for the famous Yiddish writer Isaac Bashevis Singer. Mom then began researching her grandmother's life, taking the train up to Ellis Island to search the archives for the name of the ships on which Gittle and other members of her family had journeyed to the United States. She also interviewed Gittle's two surviving children, Anna and Benjamin (her father and my grandfather) about their mother's life. Mom even dragged my dad on a trip to the Ukraine in the late 1980s, just when the Soviet Union was in collapse and Mikhail Gorbachev was opening Russia to the west. Tailed by the KGB at first, they managed to find the village near Kiev where Gittle, by then a married woman, had lived with her husband and growing brood. (The KGB desisted after realizing my parents were not spies, merely hapless Americans searching for their ancestral roots.)

In writing the book, Mom threw in a few novelistic embellishments to flesh out the facts she had gathered. She then tried half-heartedly to get the book published but as a first-time writer of fiction, she was having difficulty finding an agent. I talked to some writer friends of mine and eventually hooked her up with an elderly gent who still had contacts in the publishing industry. But he was unable to sell the book. We then reached out to several independent presses. One Jewish press expressed interest and asked if everything in the book was factual. Mom answered truthfully that she had fictionalized a few of the details and we never heard back from them.

After she died, I rediscovered the unpublished novel on her desktop and convinced my siblings that we should self-publish it. It needed a lot of line editing—in her final years, she had muddied some of the original prose. In places, the book also needed greater elaboration on the rabidly anti-Semitic policies in Russian-controlled Ukraine at the turn of the century. I undertook that task while waiting to hear back on my own manuscript. Working on Mom's book helped assuage some of the guilt I felt at not being at her bedside during the last days of her life. I have to admit that I also enjoyed editing an historical narrative that couldn't have been more different from the gritty world I had immersed myself in for the sex work book.

When I finally heard back from Phyllis Deutsch, she said she liked the manuscript but needed to find a peer reviewer to pass muster on it (since UPNE was an academic press.) With my help, she finally did: a professor of sociology at George Washington University who had extensively studied the sex industry. He gave the book a thumbs' up, writing that the manuscript was "well-written, engaging, packed with insights and interesting stories, nicely integrating academic work with the author's interview material."

While my book was getting copy edited and readied for publication, I worked with Amazon's self-publishing subsidiary on designing the cover for Mom's book. We self-published *Gittle: A Girl of the Steppes* by Estelle Rubin Brager in April 2015. To my delight, the book received some very positive notice from reviewers on Amazon. Maggie Anton, who wrote the bestselling Rashi's Daughters series, called the book, "a well-done Jewish version of *Little House on the Prairie*." Anton wrote:

> For many American Jewish women, this book's niche audience, Gittle could be their ancestress. Maybe I've missed them, but I'm not aware of other shtetl novels told from a woman's Point of View, especially not a memoir. I definitely enjoyed, and recommend this book.

I just wished Mom had been alive to read those reviews and see her book in print.

My own book was scheduled for publication that October. Phyllis Deutsch insisted on titling it, *Getting Screwed: Sex Workers and the Law*. I wasn't crazy about the title, thinking it a bit crass and likely to turn off more conservative media and reviewers (which it undoubtedly did.) But Phyllis loved the double entendre in the title, and I lost that battle.

In the weeks after my book's release that fall, I gave six book talks, one in Morgantown, two in the Boston area, one in Washington, D.C., one in Baltimore, and one in California, the epicenter of the sex workers rights movement. My most memorable appearance was at Red Emma's, a progressive book store and café in Baltimore managed by a worker's cooperative and dedicated to issues of social justice. The manager of Red Emma's had reached out to me after hearing about my book and since my younger son and his girlfriend were then living in Baltimore (Dina was going to school at Johns Hopkins and Jake was working in D.C.) I jumped at the opportunity to see them and also promote my book.

To my surprise, nearly a hundred people, most of them millennials, jammed into Red Emma's for my talk, and a cameraman from C-Span turned up and filmed my entire talk for C-Span's Book TV series. After my prepared remarks, I opened up the floor to a Q&A. While most of the questioners were very thoughtful and seemed sympathetic to the points I tried to make in my talk, one woman who came to the microphone was distinctly hostile.

"I feel like you're denigrating the sex trafficking issue," she said. "Baltimore is a port city and it's actually a huge problem here. The Shared House of Hope is a really wonderful resource for trafficking victims. I don't think this issue should be dismissed or swept under the rug."

As a journalist, I had long ago developed a thick skin and learned not take things personally. It was clear my interlocutor, a heavyset young woman wearing a big baseball cap, had come to throw cold water on my talk. But I managed to keep my cool.

"I'm sorry you got the impression that I was dismissing it or sweeping it under the rug, because I certainly wasn't," I began. "What I was saying is that yes, trafficking exists and it is a problem. But the statistics about it have been grossly inflated and falsehoods have been spread. My main argument is that with the anti-trafficking laws we have right now, the money goes into law enforcement instead of into social services. My contention is that what [trafficking victims] need is help with education, counseling, support services, and housing. What they don't need is to get re-arrested and re-traumatized by the criminal justice system, which is what is happening right now with the focus on trafficking."

A little later, another young woman came to the microphone and identified herself as a sex worker. "I do agree with a lot of what you're saying but I'd kind of like to know about your motivations behind writing this book. Knowing that your whiteness and academic credentials will get you heard over a lot of voices of sex workers, what makes you qualified to come here and talk on behalf of sex workers when it doesn't seem to be a community you're part of?"

I'd already heard this line of attack before from a few sex work activists who didn't think I was entitled to write or talk about sex work because I wasn't a sex worker. It was kind of like saying that white authors couldn't write books about slavery or men couldn't write about women. I responded:

"Well, I'm not qualified to talk on behalf of sex workers. I consider myself first and foremost a journalist and what I like to do, as I said before, is expose misleading information and stories that aren't getting told. And try to right wrongs and bring change, important policy change to issues that aren't getting attention. So that was my motivation for writing this book, my only motivation."

I took one more question after that and wrapped up by thanking everyone for coming to hear me out. I was gratified by the wave of applause that greeted me and very grateful that the evening was over.

In the ensuing weeks, not many mainstream media had the courage to review my book—perhaps the title put them off—but those that did had only positive things to say. I was particularly heartened by what reviewers for the *Los Angeles Times* and WBUR radio, the NPR affiliate in Boston, had to say. Here's an excerpt of the WBUR review:

> While expertly interlacing research and statistics with the true stories of sex workers in America, Getting Screwed wakes us all to an obscure truth: Most (but distinctly, not all) sex workers join the trade by choice, largely for economic reasons. With gripping narrative, the book reminds readers that sex workers are just as human as anyone else—only working a job deemed shameful and made dangerous by the very policymakers who pledge to protect all constituents.

In February 2016, the *Los Angeles Times* published an op-ed piece I had written about how closing down websites that allow sex worker advertisements only made sex work more dangerous for everyone and did nothing to curb trafficking. The director of the Gender and Sexuality program at California State University saw that article and invited me to come out to Los Angeles in May and give a talk to his students. He provided a generous honorarium, but the best part of that trip was spending time with my oldest son, David, who drove up from San Diego (where he was doing a legal internship) and showed me around LA.

Later that summer, on our way back from the Vineyard, my husband and I visited Bryn Gweled. I wanted to go through the archives there since I was thinking of writing about growing up on the homestead and how it had shaped me. Several long-time BG members met me one Sunday morning in the newly refurbished archives room on the second floor of the community center.

Jim Michener, whose parents had been founding members of BG and who had returned to live here after retiring a few years ago, handed me a stapled sheaf of papers titled "The Beginnings of Bryn Gweled Homesteads."

I peered at the yellowed pieces of paper. "What is this?"

"It's a transcript of an interview your father recorded with some of the original members of Bryn Gweled back in the fifties," Jim said. "I think you'll find it interesting."

I'd seen the transcript once before when I did a piece for the *Boston Globe* magazine on Bryn Gweled and other intentional communities. But I had not read it closely at the time. Now I looked at it with fresh eyes. Most of the Q&A focused on the nuts and bolts of how the founders of Bryn Gweled discovered and purchased the two hundred and forty acres of undulating hills in Bucks County and set about building a unique community here. But one comment from a founding member made my eyebrows shoot up. It came from Edward Ramberg, a research physicist who worked at RCA and had helped invent the first electron microscope. Ramberg, in responding to a question my dad asked about why most of the houses in BG ended up being architecturally modern, said:

> Our houses were largely unconventional because our whole approach was unconventional. We questioned the validity of authority, whether it was the authority of the government asking us to take part in war or the authority of custom proscribing [our] styles of living and spending leisure time.

Wow. It suddenly dawned on me that I had spent much of my life doing just that. I had questioned authority in almost every story I did as a journalist and had done the same with both of my books. The publication of *Side Effects* had brought about real policy change.

Researchers' financial ties with the pharmaceutical industry now had to be publicly disclosed and many medical institutions had tightened their conflict-of-interest policies. And here I was stirring the pot again with my second book, *Getting Screwed: Sex Workers and the Law*, which offered a decidedly anti-establishment view of prostitution. My sex work book had brought me full circle with themes that framed much of my career: exposing sexual exploitation and the marginalization of vulnerable individuals. And to think that hiding in plain sight all this time was a transcript of an interview that my own father had done sixty years prior, an interview that helped explain why I had become the person I did. I felt simultaneously lightheaded and complete.

That afternoon, when we left Bryn Gweled to head home, I was still on a high from what I had discovered in the archives. On our way out of the homestead, I noticed that the grass, the trees, indeed the entire landscape, was so mesmerizingly green that it felt like I had stepped into a fantastical Emerald countryside that surely could only exist in the movies. All I could see was green and it was a breathtakingly peaceful sight.

Acknowledgements

This book would not have been possible without the encouragement and support of many friends, relatives, and colleagues who helped me find my voice. The narrative is constructed from detailed journals I kept over the years, letters exchanged with family and friends, as well as notes I took as a working journalist and my published body of work. It is also based on the recollections of family and friends as well as my own. I am grateful to the members of my writing group who read early drafts and encouraged me to keep going, wise souls like Lois Raimondo, Mary Kay McFarland, Benyamin Cohen and John Temple. I am especially grateful to Jim Harms, Adriana Paramo and Inon Shampanier who gave me insightful suggestions on how to shape the narrative. And I owe a great debt to my son, David Palmer Aronlee, whose sharp eye and smart sense of craft, helped me refine each chapter and flesh out my story.

I would also like to thank the talented production team at Bedazzled Ink Publishing for their help, including C.A. Casey for her incisive edits, Elizabeth Gibson for her superb marketing guidance, and Sapling Studio for their snappy cover design.

Alison Bass is an award-winning journalist and the author of two critically acclaimed nonfiction books: *Getting Screwed, Sex Workers and the Law* (2015) and *Side Effects: A Prosecutor, a Whistleblower and a Bestselling Antidepressant on Trial*. (2008). *Side Effects* received the prestigious National Association of Science Writers' Science in Society Award and the film rights to Side Effects have been optioned.

Bass recently retired as Associate Professor of Journalism at West Virginia University. She was a long-time science and medical writer for *The Boston Globe* and a series she wrote for *The Globe* was nominated for a Pulitzer Prize in the Public Service category. Her articles and essays have also appeared in *The Los Angeles Times, Buzzfeed, The Village Voice, Psychology Today*, and numerous other media. She has received a number of journalism awards for her work, including an Alicia Patterson Fellowship and the Top Media Award from the National Mental Health Association. For more on her credentials, please visit her website at www.alison-bass.com.